Dedication

To Jeff Friedrichsen,
who truly is the man I always wanted.

Contents

Acknowledgments

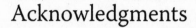

First and foremost, to my literary agent Bill Jensen for his creativity, guidance, and friendship. I'm so thankful that he finally said yes.

To all my friends at Multnomah Publishers, especially Bonnie Johnson, Steffany Woolsey, Tiffany Lauer, Doug Gabbert, Guy Coleman, Gayle Sawyer, and the many others who have worked long and hard on my behalf.

To Peggy Stovesand, my fabulous first draft editor. I'm grateful for her friendship, honesty, and hard work on the rough draft of my manuscript.

I want to acknowledge the many women who shared their private, and sometimes painful, stories with me. This book was a group effort, and I am eternally grateful for their transparency.

To my family, especially my mother, Lorraine Garner, and my sisters, Linda Shipman and Karen Brahney, for providing wisdom, insight, and precious little pieces of their own lives.

To my wonderfully supportive church family at Church on the Mountain. They prayed, they encouraged, and they cheered me on.

To my circle of girlfriends. I am thankful for the laughter, friendship, lunches at Good Life Café, long walks, prayer, and fellowship that we share.

To Marita Littauer and the gang at CLAS Services—they have opened significant doors in my speaking and writing career, and I thank them.

Last but not least, to my husband, Jeff, and our children, Andrew and Amy. I thank them for their patience and encouragement during the writing of this book.

Introduction

DID YOU KNOW that even failure can have value in God's economy? When a life has been redeemed by His grace, when a marriage has been restored by His goodness, it must be told.

And for that reason, this book begins with my story of failure almost fifteen years ago. But bear in mind, the point of my story is not that I failed. We all fail at times, in one degree or another. The point is that I got back up. Emotionally bruised and spiritually shaken, I took steps to seek forgiveness and restoration from God.

He did forgive, and He restored me—and so much more! He gave me a message to share with women. He gave me a passion to see them protected from making the same mistake I did. He infused within me the longing to see women's eyes opened to the truth that their heart's desire is often no further away than the big lug lying next to them in bed each night.

You may not be married to Prince Charming. But then, no one is—except Cinderella! In a world that idolizes the airbrushed fantasies found on *People* magazine's Sexiest Man

Alive lists, we *must* sit up and notice the unique qualities of the guys we are married to.

Marriage can be difficult at times. You may be feeling crushed by the weight of unresolved arguments, still reeling from the sting of illness or depression, or facing a union completely devoid of romance. Perhaps your husband has simply been in a bad mood for the last twelve years. I don't know the exact level of discomfort you are experiencing. But I can tell you that God is supernatural—and nothing is beyond His reach. Bring to Him what faith you have, even if it is only the size of a mustard seed. Dare to believe that God has something more for you.

Think of this book as a new lens, a "heavenly perspective" through which to view your husband. At first, things may seem a little out of focus and unfamiliar. But pretty soon you'll find yourself seeing your husband with new eyes. And with clarity and insight you'll start to identify those qualities that were hidden under the layers of busyness, irritations, or bitterness.

I call this the "ta-da!" factor, and it has the potential to bless your life dramatically. The "ta-da!" factor does not come after your husband loses thirty-five pounds, or goes through extensive therapy, or agrees to buy that new home you've been hoping for. Instead, it comes when the Lord shows you just *who* you are married to.

Along with the realization of this blessing that has been right under your nose all along, joy bubbles up from a place long dormant. You are renewed, and your marriage is renewed, too. With your new lens, you'll see that even in an imperfect world, with an imperfect guy, living out an imperfect marriage—you serve a perfect God. A God who delights in making all things new...who delights in reminding you of His blessings. A God who shows you plainly that the man you always wanted is the one you already have!

the man you always wanted

is

the one you already have

Here I stand,
　　Seeds of hope long ago sown,
Lovingly cultivated by an expert Hand,
　　Brought to maturity,
Now fully grown.

A weapon formed against me,
　　To steal, kill, and destroy,
I now advance as David did,
　　Wielding the giant's own sword,
To cut off the head of the enemy's lies,
　　I come against him
In the Name of the Lord.

Yesterday is past,
　　Behold, all things are new!
His mercies are my song,
　　And like a radiant sunrise,
I now proclaim New Mercies to you!

Written in collaboration with Bethany Hicks

1

Playing with Fire

I LOVED MY NEW CHURCH. It was vibrant, exciting, and contemporary. When the pastor preached, the Bible came alive to me as never before. He was like no other speaker I had ever heard, and my excitement held no bounds. I felt like I had won the lottery just to be able to attend this extraordinary church.

In addition to his marvelous preaching, this pastor could compose and sing music beautifully. I remember how sometimes during the Sunday service he would spontaneously walk over to the piano and begin worshipping the Lord in song while running his hands over the ivory keys. He would bring the congregation along as he led the way into astonishing worship.

My husband, Jeff, was starting a new job, so we had just relocated to this new city. Although he was not a Christian at the time, Jeff was supportive of my desire to get involved in a new church. I quickly made friends and started serving in different areas of church life, such as planning retreats for the ladies, helping in the nursery, and eventually even preaching and teaching on occasion.

This period in my life represented a wonderful awakening to the presence and reality of God. There were days when I literally could not stop smiling as I went about my daily chores. God was so real to me. He was making His Word come alive to me...and I was being changed. I was falling more and more in love with Jesus. I was also beginning to get a glimpse of my future, which clearly seemed to include a call to the ministry. Like a brilliant sunrise, Christ took my breath away with His presence and promises. My new church and my new pastor were being used by God to facilitate these remarkable changes in my life.

I was a happily married woman, a doting mom, and a strong Christian. That's why nothing could have prepared me for what came next.

A Too-Close Friendship

Over time, I developed a close relationship with the pastor and his wife, along with several others in the church congregation. My new friends and I would get together regularly for picnics while our kids ran around and played together. What fun we had discussing the things of God, enjoying mutual excitement over our wonderful church and what God was doing there. We planned for the future and anticipated many years of exciting and productive times of ministry together.

Jeff was seldom a part of these get-togethers, as he was working during the day. But during this time he was accepting of the amount of time I was spending with my new friends.

One of the most exciting events at our church each week was the Sunday night service. The worship team was let loose, and without the constraints of time, the sounds of adoration and praise would fill the sanctuary for as long as an hour. After that, the congregation was invited to take turns sharing what God was doing in their lives. The pastor would then preach for a while, and we would end the service with prayer.

These Sunday night meetings would go on for hours. The presence of God was so *real.* God was manifesting Himself, and nobody wanted to leave. We would eventually take pity on the poor nursery workers and end the meeting somewhere between 10 and 11 p.m.

Who wanted to go home after that? I sure didn't! So a big group of us would then head over to the local Denny's restaurant to enjoy each other's company and have some lively conversation. We would laugh and talk, and relive the extraordinary church service that had just taken place.

There were many evenings that winter when I would call my husband just before we went into the restaurant, to see if he minded my going. Now, my conscience minded my going… the Holy Spirit who lives inside me minded my going…and even my common sense minded my going. But no, I had to call to see if my husband (who had now been alone for the last five hours) minded my going.

As I stood outside Denny's in the darkened phone booth, I could hear in his voice that he *did* mind my going. His voice said *okay*, but his tone whispered *no.* I chose to ignore that. It was one of many red lights that I eventually drove right through.

More Red Lights

Over that winter and into early spring I found myself spending more time socializing with the pastor and his wife. Sometimes my husband would be included, such as at dinner parties or sporting events, but many times I would just hang out with the pastor and his wife in their home without him. Jeff was being increasingly isolated from my new life.

As the spring days grew warmer, the pastor's wife and I began spending a lot time together. She was such good company, and our friendship grew steadily. She seemed to have no awareness of the developing flirtation between her husband and me.

Many times when the pastor's wife and I were having lunch at her home, her husband would drop by for a few hours and we would chat. Our personalities were similar, so of course we found each other charming, witty, and irresistibly funny. We could laugh and talk for hours.

I received great pleasure and validation from my relationship with the pastor. I was flattered by his friendship, feeling a type of approval and affirmation that I had never known. The inordinate amount of attention I was receiving swelled my ego, causing me to become somewhat self-absorbed.

By the time summer arrived, we had begun talking on the phone regularly, expanding our relationship beyond the already too-loose boundaries. He began calling me each day while his wife took an afternoon nap with their children. Of course Jeff had no idea that the pastor and I were chatting regularly—this was something I was hiding from him.

This seemed wrong...I *knew* it was wrong. But there I went, speeding through another red light.

Then came the dream.

In my dream I saw the pastor come around the corner of a building. As he approached me, I heard the voice of the Lord above and behind me saying, "You are spending too much time together!" I sat bolt upright in bed, knowing I had just had an encounter with God. I was literally shaking with fear.

I called up my trusted friend Debbie, who was a mentor and older sister in the Lord. She listened as I told her all that had been happening in my life. I held nothing back, doing my best to be as transparent with her as possible.

Her counsel was that I leave that church immediately. During our long, tearful conversation, she literally begged me to get out of the pastor's life *that day*, and to run to a different church—as if my life depended on it. She rebuked me in no uncertain terms and corrected me like a mother in the Lord.

I vowed that I would obey. I promised to do exactly as she said. I pledged to extract myself from this man's life quickly.

But I did not. I chose not to.

You see, at first I was convinced that Debbie's advice was 100 percent correct. Then, little by little, I decided that I could handle the pastor's escalating attention. Leaving a church I loved so dearly seemed too drastic.

I would make a concerted effort to put some distance between the pastor and myself. How hard could that be? I loved my husband. In my heart of hearts, I knew that I would never betray his trust. Jeff was a wonderful man—hard working, kind, so good to our son. So what was the problem here? Nothing, really...just a little harmless flirting, that's all.

So on I went, careening recklessly through another red light.

All hell broke loose one hot July afternoon. My little boy was napping, and I was having my daily chat on the phone with the pastor...when he revealed his interest in me as more than just a friend.

Thus began the worst season of my life. I had played with fire, enjoying the attention and flirting shamelessly, and now I was getting burned. I had no intention of leaving my husband. I had no intention of having a sexual fling with this man. I was just enjoying a little harmless flattery, a perk of being the pastor's favorite "sheep." But now I was in deep trouble, and I felt guilty for not following Debbie's advice from weeks before.

I didn't know how to get out of the mess I had made of my life. There were many times when God had tried to stop my descent. So many times He had tried to correct me. But I chose not to give up my relationship with the pastor...or his wife...or the many church members that I had grown to love so deeply over the years. I chose not to give up all the fun and fellowship that came with attending the church.

Bottom line, I chose not to relinquish the emotional attention I received from my inappropriate friendship with the pastor.

Exposure: The Ticket for Running Red Lights

The church was run by a board of three elders and their wives, in addition to the pastor and his wife. By late summer the elders got wind of the fact that there was a too-close friendship going on between the pastor and me, and they took action to see that it went no further. At the elders' request, I met with them and was asked at that time to leave the church permanently.

The thing I remember most about that meeting was the unconditional love I felt in the room. It was the tangible love of God. I knew the elders were doing their best to prayerfully handle this uncomfortable situation, and God in His love confirmed their decision.

You may wonder if the pastor was also asked to leave the church. Yes, eventually the elders decided that this would be the best course of action for all involved, and the pastor and his family relocated to a different city.

The church survived, but it was never again the same. The damage was irreversible, the breach irreparable; many people were deeply wounded as a result of our actions.

Shortly after that meeting with the elders, I came clean with my husband about the whole ugly situation. To say he was disappointed would be an understatement. Jeff was understandably hurt and angry, but he forgave me. And ultimately, he took comfort knowing that nothing had happened physically between the pastor and me.

From Gossip and Despair to Forgiveness and Healing

The church members responded with a range of emotions: sadness, rage, and concern, to name a few. Some reacted by gossiping; others, by praying.

I understood all these reactions. In a way, I felt I deserved the ugliness being directed toward me...but that didn't make it any easier.

It was at this time that the most incredible thing happened. As I began focusing on the relationships in my own home, my husband became my best friend. While blame, accusations, and rumors were being tossed around our small town like grenades, my husband was a shelter for me, a steady source of comfort and forgiveness.

Why had I never noticed this side of Jeff before? He was gracious, loyal, merciful, and exceedingly kind. The enemy had tried his best to turn my head with the attentions of another man, and all along I was missing the depth, worth, and desirability of the man I already had.

It took time, but my marriage recovered. Eventually it grew stronger, happier, and more genuine. I realized just how much I loved Jeff—*really* loved him. In time we moved to another city and found a new church, and that was when my husband became a Christian.

I came away from that time in my life convinced of two truths:

TRUTH #1: *Many women grow cold to the wonderful attributes that first draw them to their husbands.*

Familiarity, the cares of this life, and the enemy can obscure the qualities women once admired in their husbands. As a conference speaker, I minister to women who are blindly trudging through marriage, thinking maybe the grass is greener on the other side of the fence. But the reality is that sometimes there's a garbage dump on the other side of the fence.

After my flirtatious and destructive friendship with the pastor ended, I *ran* for the safety and security of my husband. It was as if the clouds had parted on a deeply overcast day and the sun shone brightly for the first time in months. With complete clarity I comprehended my admiration, desire, and love for Jeff—and it has only deepened with time.

Several years ago at a conference, I counseled a young woman who was growing disappointed in her marriage. She wasn't sure she had married the right guy, they weren't getting along, and she was regretting her choice. I happened to know this couple, and I knew firsthand what a terrific guy he was. I reminded her that although she did not see her husband as a "prize," other women might very well be looking at her life with envy, seeing the wonderful, handsome, smart guy that she had the privilege of marrying. I counseled her to wake up and appreciate the man she was taking for granted.

Think about it this way. For the divorce rate to be as high as it is, we basically have well-intentioned but deeply flawed men and women switching partners for their own personal happiness. The sentiment seems to be, "I'll divorce my imperfect and annoying husband and marry the imperfect and annoying husband of my friend."

Since there is no perfect person out there, and exchanging partners doesn't fix the problem, what is the answer?

It's recognizing the truth that the man you always wanted is the man you already have, that the big lug lying next to you each night really is your Prince Charming. And I believe this truth best becomes a reality in our lives as we are invested in an engaging and joyful relationship with the Savior.

TRUTH #2: *The approval we long for will be found only in our relationship with Christ, not in the acceptance and favor of other men.*

I began that arduous season devoted to Christ and my husband, but I was drawn away by my pride and a refusal to obey the Lord's warnings. Every disobedient step led me further from Him. And every time I turned a deaf ear to God's rebuke, I wandered a little further down the path of destruction. By the end of the ordeal I was actually faking the presence of God, "playing church"—just going through the motions when it came to ministry.

In the same way that I returned to the safety and security of my marriage after the inappropriate relationship with the pastor, I also ran quickly to the protection of my first love,

Jesus. It was in that place of repentance and prayer that I remembered God *is* my "all in all." He is more than enough.

What I discovered about that ordeal is this: *It's only as I am found in Christ that I can be content in my relationship with my husband.* If I'm fulfilled, it's not because Jeff came through the door last night with a dozen long-stemmed red roses, a love poem, and a box of candy. Rather, I'm fulfilled by the ultimate Lover of my soul.

This leads to great contentment. And because I am deeply contented in the quietest and most secret places of my heart, by the love and approval of Christ, I can then reach out in love to my husband and receive his love freely. Best of all, I can put my expectations where they properly belong—on the shoulders of the Lord.

How about you? Are your expectations for a happy life and fulfilling marriage placed squarely on the shoulders of God? If you're anything like me, you may be tempted to make your husband responsible for your personal happiness; or the lack thereof, his transgression.

But there are really only two viable sources of hope for your marriage. The first is prayer: taking your concerns daily and laying them in faith at the feet of Christ. And the second is *you*. While you can't control your husband's actions, you can control your own. That should greatly encourage you, because with it comes hope! Change is possible. Change is imminent. Change is coming…do you feel it?

As you journey through the next nine chapters, you'll be faced with some choices. Honesty…transparency…forgiveness…surrender…discovery…revelation…faith. These are just a few of the responses that must come. But I promise you, it will be worth it. Think of the time you spend reading this book as a well-planned-out and exciting pilgrimage. This journey will have moments of insight, sparkling brilliantly like ocean waters on a clear day. Other moments will be rocky, dislodging deeply embedded negative thinking.

On this journey you will encounter the sweet fragrance of memory, recalling the reasons you fell in love with your husband in the first place.

And in the end, the pilgrimage will return you to the beginning, to the place where your marriage started—first love.

2

Culture Shock

Snuggled under a down throw, I cradle a bowl of ice cream on my lap while Jeff and I watch television. Suddenly, without warning, we go from viewing a family-friendly program to being sexually assaulted. The assailant? A writhing supermodel showcasing Barely There underwear for Victoria's Secret. Obviously a very limber girl, the contortionist positions her body in numerous sexually explicit, almost pornographic poses. She is clad in less fabric then it would take to patch the knee of my daughter's jeans.

• ◆ •

My little girl, Amy, and I sit together in front of my computer composing a letter to her pen pal in Nigeria. The ad space on my Hotmail account displays a curvaceous young woman wearing a bikini so tiny that she must have had to endure quite the waxing for *that* photo shoot. She's helping to advertise a cyber-dating website, where all applicants are supposedly screened in order to sift out the riffraff. Her lips are parted seductively, her eyes smolder with passion, and her body language conveys that she is waiting eagerly for Mr. Right.

• ◆ •

As I make beds and help my family get out the door in the morning, I switch on *Good Morning America* to catch up on the world at large. The more disturbing news stories include another massive hurricane heading straight for Florida; the rising death toll from the recent earthquake in Pakistan; and the update on the bird flu pandemic. But it isn't until the commercials that I literally have to lunge for the remote. What prompts this? A commercial featuring a popular crime show. The worst part isn't the bloody and mutilated body of the victim, but rather the overtly sensual love scene: an almost naked man unhooking the bra of his lover. As her bra falls to the ground, I race to turn it off.

• ◆ •

The world in which we now live is unlike any other time in history. As we look back in time, there is absolutely *nothing* to compare it to. Technology has advanced to such an extent that anyone, anywhere, can now partake in a variety of previously forbidden sexual fulfillments. The catch phrase "It's all good" has come to define this generation.

But truth be told, it's *not* "all good." Sin is increasing, hearts are growing cold, marriages are failing, and lives are crumbling. Christ, describing the "end of the age," tells us in Matthew 24:12–13: "Because of the increase of wickedness, the love of most will grow cold, but he who stands firm to the end will be saved."

Hurry Up and Throw It Away

We live in a disposable society. It's now cheaper to buy a new toaster, vacuum, blender, TV, or computer than it is to have the old one repaired. Our frantic pace and propensity for purchasing new things dictates that we toss out anything old and obsolete, replacing it with something shiny and appealing.

This attitude has crossed over into modern-day marriage. Elizabeth Taylor started it...Tom Cruise and Brad Pitt did it... so why not me?

Twenty-first-century culture downplays the value of marriage. It can be challenging to cultivate faithful behavior when the commentary of our society is summed up on shows like *Desperate Housewives* and *Sex in the City*. How can the average woman experience contentment in her marriage when so many people today justify illicit sexual behavior just by ogling their favorite TV shows?

Society places great value on the first stages of thrilling romantic love, as well as the passionate physical pursuits that usually follow. However, the beginning stages of romantic love cannot lay claim to the treasures found in a longstanding, committed marriage. This chapter is going to shed light on how fulfilling married love can be.

While married love may not always burn with the heat and passion of that first stage of romantic love, neither does married love burn out easily. And the consistent warmth it provides is there on the coldest of days and darkest of nights.

The Different Facets of Married Love

Many years ago, my dear friend Sarah went through some devastating trials in her marriage when her husband of twenty-five years betrayed her trust in some alarming and shocking ways. As Sarah's world spiraled out of control, divorce became not only a defensible but recommended resolution.

However, Sarah remained committed to her husband. Why? For several key reasons. First and foremost, Sarah's husband sought her forgiveness and was willing to do whatever it took to reconcile. Second, Sarah and her husband shared twenty-five years of memories.

You may be tempted to scorn the latter as inadequate. But don't underestimate the depth and beauty of a love filled with memories.

When Sarah and David married, she was nineteen and pregnant, and he was a lanky twenty-two-year-old. With the odds stacked against them, they made their way in the world—together. Twenty-five years later, no one but David remembered what Sarah looked like at nineteen, or knew what it felt like to start a marriage with the added stress of pregnancy. No one else understood the laughter and secrets they shared in those first years. No one else could ever appreciate how hard they worked to stay together in those difficult beginning years.

David knew all the stories…because he was *in* all the stories. Together they designed and built a home, raised three children, took family camping trips, planned and paid for all three of their daughters' weddings, and survived a bout with cancer. They cared for and eventually buried their elderly parents. They threw parties, took trips to the beach, disciplined naughty kids, and weathered financial hardships through the lean years. They fought…they laughed…they prayed…they cried. No one else was woven into Sarah's life like David.

This is a love full of memories. This is a love worth fighting for. In the midst of marital devastation, Sarah chose to fight.

Many years have passed since then, and I can confirm that it was a wise choice on Sarah's part. She and David have grown older together. They have a depth of comfort, companionship, and love that comes only from a marriage that has weathered life's storms.

Standing on the precipice of the life-and-death struggle for her marriage, Sarah discovered that the man she always wanted was the one she already had.

In today's disposable society, it has becoming increasingly rare to see people persevere through the rough spots of marriage. "Personal happiness" is the garish banner waving over our lives, as we blithely remove any and every obstacle that stands in the way of this pursuit. But true love is worth fighting for. Married love is worth fighting for.

Last week I sat on the floor of my den and looked at family pictures for over three hours. We're in the process of moving, and my plan was to simply box up my twenty or so photo albums and move on to the next project. But one thing led to another, and I found myself carried along on the photographic journey of Jeff and Paula Friedrichsen.

A bride dressed in white and a handsome groom, saying their vows before God and man...

Daddy mowing the lawn while his son follows behind with a little plastic mower, "helping" his father...

A very pregnant wife standing in front of the Christmas tree, her husband's strong arm wrapped around her...

Father and daughter walking along the beach holding hands, a Hawaiian sunset blazing behind them.

The pictures went on and on, telling our story. There were birthday parties and large family gatherings. Twenty-pound

Thanksgiving turkeys and crisp winter days of sledding. Just a normal little life. But what a treasure there is in sharing a normal little life together.

If you are struggling with boredom in your marriage and a crushing sense of "average," it can be easy to discount the treasure of a "shared life." But I encourage you to get out those old photo albums and take a trip down memory lane—relishing, embracing, and celebrating a "love full of memories."

1. The Facet of Prevailing Love

Erica Kane has been married *ten* times. Although she's just a fictional character on *All My Children*, it's still pretty outlandish behavior, even for a cheesy daytime soap opera. Frankly, Erica's behavior makes most of our marriages look darn good by comparison.

Adultery, fornication, and divorce are served up weekly on TV, like arsenic wrapped in puff pastry, served on a sterling silver tray. Some of the most base and immoral primetime shows are superbly cast, scripted, and produced. They have at their disposal the coolest and most fashionable clothes, the skinniest actresses, the most handsome actors, and the best writers in the industry. And if we aren't discerning, we may find ourselves eating, digesting, and being subtly changed by the poison.

You've picked up this book because you value your marriage. In a world where good is called bad and bad is called good, you're looking for answers. Thankfully, we can look to the Word of God for solutions to this present-day marriage quagmire.

Is there such a thing as enduring, prevailing love? What

does the Bible have to say about it? In 1 Corinthians 13:4–8 we read:

> Love is patient, love is kind. It does not envy, it does not boast, it is not proud. It is not rude, it is not self-seeking, it is not easily angered, it keeps no record of wrongs. Love does not delight in evil but rejoices with the truth. It always protects, always trusts, always hopes, always perseveres. Love never fails.

God's love is prevailing, and the love He gives us for our spouses can be prevailing and enduring as well.

After many years of marriage, my friend Trudy's heart had grown a bit dull toward her husband. It's not that he was a bad guy. On the contrary—he was a good provider, a loving husband and father, and a nice-looking man. But life has a way of making an unforgettable guy seem forgettable. In the busyness of running a successful business and raising a gaggle of kids, they had simply grown apart.

Trudy recognized this as a real problem in her marriage, so she did what she always does: She ran to God, in prayer, for answers.

One day God answered her prayer in a tangible way. Trudy had gone into their home office to tell Jack something when she noticed for the first time in many years how blue and sparkling her husband's eyes were. As she stood there looking at him, she was struck by just how cute Jack was. All of a sudden, Trudy was physically drawn to her husband. She was reminded of the intoxicating pleasure of having sex with Jack.

Passion was renewed and reignited in her marriage that day. Trudy took a long look at Jack with fresh eyes—and what she saw was a gift from God.

While the passionate side of enduring love is wonderful

and important, this kind of love is much more than just physical. In fact, *Roget's Thesaurus* tells us that the word *endure* means "to sustain, withstand, undergo, weather, and to experience." A prevailing and enduring love is built over a lifetime and is more valuable than almost any other accomplishment in life. Because in the end, enduring love willingly undergoes suffering for the sake of the beloved.

In his sermon "It's Friday, but Sunday's Coming," Tony Campolo shares the moving story of the death of the mother of his friend Darrel Moody, a theologian who teaches at Southern Seminary.

Tony recounts how, as Darrel's mother finished breakfast one morning, she slumped in her chair and passed out. Darrel's father gathered up his wife, plunked her in his pickup, and tore off down the street like a teenager in a hotrod. Unfortunately, at the hospital she was pronounced dead on arrival.

After the funeral, Darrel, his brother, and their father retreated back to the porch of Darrel's homestead where they talked and talked as daylight faded into evening. Suddenly the old man said, "Take me back to the cemetery!" The sons replied, "It's too late."

But Darrel's dad insisted. "Take me back—take me back to the cemetery!"

After Darrel's dad checked out the grave with a flashlight, he stepped back and said, "It's been a good life and it ended just the way I wanted it to end—she died first."

Then he gathered his sons in his arms and held them tightly. Finally he said, "We can go home now. We can go—it's been a good day...it's been a very good day."

Prevailing love reaches beyond the grave and presses past grief. The old man in the story above actually received comfort in the midst of his mourning, just by knowing that his beloved wife did not have to endure the suffering of losing him first. Where romantic passion fades, enduring love steadfastly remains—to the grave, and even beyond.

2. The Facet of Comfortable Love

Comfortable love is like coming home after a hard day's work to the smell of beef stew simmering in the Crock-Pot. Comfortable love is like changing out of a business suit, nylons, and high heels into flannel jammies and fluffy slippers. Comfortable love is like coming in from a raging winter storm to a cozy home warmed by a crackling fire.

In a day and age where the siren song of modern media promises women true and lasting happiness based on their income, material possessions, bust size, or hair color—marriage offers us *comfortable love.*

Yesterday was Jeff's and my twenty-first wedding anniversary. We will go out to dinner next Saturday night to celebrate, and then snuggle on the couch to watch a movie together. And this is perfect. This is enough. This is my marriage.

You may be underwhelmed by our celebration plans. Maybe you're wondering, *Where's the trip to Paris?* or *Where's the diamond anniversary band?* (You know...like on the Zales commercial.) Or *Won't there be a surprise getaway to a cozy bed and breakfast, where Jeff has arranged for chilled champagne and draws you a bubble bath?*

Uh...no. You see, that's just not Jeff's style. But he more than makes up for it. Because while unrealistic expectations and perfection in body and home are foisted upon women at every turn, my husband accepts me as I am. In a culture where an extreme makeover promises us fulfillment and happiness, my husband offers lasting love and enduring security.

Now, that's not to say I don't do my best to stay fit, trim, shaved, and dyed—because I do! I'm as vain as the next girl. But comfortable love does not dictate that I make a mad dash from the bed to the bathroom so that I can "put on my face" before greeting Jeff each morning.

Yesterday morning, before he left for work, Jeff took me in his arms (ignoring my bad breath, crazy hair, scraggly jammies and all) and told me how much he loved me. He said, "You are a wonderful wife and mother—and I'm lucky to have you. Happy anniversary! I love you so much."

Warmth and security are found in the unconditional love of my husband, and I take comfort in the knowledge that I'm not still *auditioning* for the part. And while Jeff's eyes do light up when I walk into his workplace in cute jeans, with my hair curled, and wearing makeup, the true compliment is in that "everyday" love he so freely extends to me.

And I extend that same love and acceptance to Jeff. Although I appreciate the fact that he gets cleaned up and nicely dressed each day, our marriage (and our sex life) is not laid upon the foundation of physical perfection. I'll take my big lug just the way he is.

Comfortable love doesn't make comparisons. Comfortable love accepts and embraces all that your husband *is*, letting the light of your attention illuminate his good qualities. If you're in the habit of comparing your man to the likes of George Clooney—well, just stop. Right now. George has been plucked, waxed, manicured, dyed, and airbrushed (and do you really want your husband to spend more time at the beauty shop than you?).

The media rarely casts comfortable love in a good light. Instead, it's portrayed as boring and predictable. But that just isn't true! In the tumultuous time we live in, your marriage, home life, and relationship with God offer the joy, security, and *comfort* you crave.

3. The Facet of Familiar Love

There is a beautiful and poignant scene in a 1984 made-for-TV movie called *Heartsounds* that touched me deeply. Even though it has been over twenty years since I saw that movie, I will never forget the heartbreaking emotion that this particular scene invoked in me.

In the movie, Mary Tyler Moore, playing the wife of a man (James Garner) who died of a heart attack, stands in front of her husband's closet. As she contemplates what to do with his clothes, she slowly takes one of his suit jackets off the hanger and brings it to her nose, breathing in deeply. After a moment, she buries her face in his jacket, drinking in his scent, crying, remembering.... She misses him so much that she can hardly breathe, and the smell of her late husband is almost too much to take. It's comforting and agonizing, reassuring and painful.

This is familiar love.

We don't place a high enough price on familiar love. In fact, it's often scorned. As the saying goes, "Familiarity breeds contempt." But I make the assertion that familiarity breeds appreciation!

Familiar things are *good* things: the smell of morning coffee, a favorite song playing on the radio, your own bed after being away for several weeks, and most important, the man you share your life with.

You'll notice I *didn't* say, "Familiarity breeds perfection." Nothing is perfect. But familiar things are companionable, comfortable, and reassuring—like a soft, inviting pillow after a long, hard day.

My Aunt Evelyn just turned eighty. She's learned a few things along the way, and I want to share with you what she told me about "familiar love."

She and my Uncle Bill were married many years ago

under some pretty trying circumstances. Recently widowed, she was the young mother of two little girls. He was a widower raising three teenage boys on his own. Shortly after they married, Bill found himself working two hundred miles away and commuting home on weekends. This, along with Bill's pretty substantial beer habit, caused Evelyn to wonder if she had made a mistake by marrying him. His faults seemed glaring; his shortcomings, numerous.

In Evelyn's heart she knew that marriage was for better or worse, and she resolved to stay put—but that didn't stop the feelings of worry and regret that plagued her during this difficult time in her life.

It was shortly after their first year of marriage that Bill's oldest son died in a tragic accident. In Bill's overwhelming grief, he clung to his new wife. As they journeyed together through the sorrow of this loss, a deep love grew in Evelyn's heart for her husband. He needed her, she needed him, and their love was solid.

Their years together brought numerous joys and sorrows. Through them all, Bill and Evelyn grew closer—united in laughter and friendship, joined in romance and love. They could talk about everything...they could talk about nothing. His glaring faults faded away over the years, leaving behind a companionable husband. And in the end, it was all the *familiar* things about him that meant the most to Evelyn.

My aunt stood by the bed of her beloved husband as he slipped from this life into the next. There was nothing left unsaid, nothing left undone. They had loved each other well, and there were no regrets.

How quickly foolish people trade the preciousness of familiar love for the fleeting goose bumps of a casual sexual encounter. Many exchange God's gift of *familiarity* for the illicit pleasure found in steamy romance novels (where comparison becomes obsession) or the thrill of an office flirtation (and the seductive sexual innuendo that usually accompanies it).

Some have rashly tossed away the *gold* of familiar love for the *tin* of self-gratification. I don't condemn; rather, I speak from experience. It seems unthinkable to me now that I would have allowed an outsider to turn my head, even for a moment, from the treasure of the familiar love I share with my husband.

What foolish creatures we humans are! Thank God for His grace, His salvation, and His Word.

4. The Facet of Forgiving Love

Forgiving love is not romantic. It's not touchy-feely. It's not what they write love songs about. Forgiving love is not for sissies. It doesn't *feel* good. Forgiving love is for people willing to fight for their marriages. It's for the brave at heart. It's for the determined. It's perhaps the most Godlike love there is.

Susan was a woman with regrets. An early choice in her marriage changed the course of her entire life, but eventually ended up saving the marriage of her daughter-in-law.

Lou and Susan were married young, and started having kids right away. As far as Susan was concerned, Lou was the love of her life. She did her best to make a nice home for him and treat him like the king she thought he was. Unfortunately, it turned out Lou was all too human—and as we all know, humans sometimes do stupid things.

Lou decided that they should rent out the garage apartment located on their property, and Susan readily agreed. She fixed it up nice, put out a For Rent sign, and soon had a willing (if not charming) renter.

Barbara was an attractive young widow with four children, and she and Susan became fast friends. The kids had fun playing together, the women would chat, and Lou helped Barbara out by doing all the "man" stuff around the garage apartment.

As time progressed, Susan took Barbara under her wing. She wanted to help this poor widow and her fatherless children by drawing them into the warmth of their wonderful family.

Can you guess what happened next? That's right: Lou and Barbara began an affair.

The affair remained secret for some time, but Susan eventually found out. And in her shock, hurt, and despair, she grabbed her kids, a suitcase full of clothes, and ran out of the house, never to return.

So what's the problem, you say? After all, Susan had every right to leave. She was betrayed. She isn't a doormat, after all! Perhaps you applaud her choice, believing she handled the situation in the best possible way.

But I beg to differ.

You see, Lou followed Susan. He wanted his family back, and he actively sought reconciliation and forgiveness. But at the time, Susan's disappointment in the man she once called "king" was just too intense. She felt justified in her anger toward her husband (she was) and vindicated by her unforgiving attitude (she was not).

As time went on, Lou stopped pursuing Susan. He resigned himself to the idea that his mistake had ruined their marriage. He and Barbara eventually resumed their relationship and ultimately married, blending all nine children into one very large, dysfunctional family.

Susan's regret began around the time of Lou and Barbara's wedding, but by then it was too late to accept Lou's apology.

Fast-forward many years. An elderly Susan sips tea with

her daughter-in-law, Claire, and shares her story of regret and unforgivingness. She tells Claire, "If you ever discover that your husband has betrayed you, don't do *anything* at that moment. Wait...let the dust settle. Don't make any major decisions. Don't run. Be willing to forgive. Be willing to at least consider reconciliation. Take things slow."

Twenty years after receiving that sage advice from Susan, Claire needed it. Her husband had brought scandal to their home, and her emotions screamed, "Run!" But as she contemplated her next move, she told me that she heard the voice of her mother-in-law repeat those wise words.

And so Claire stayed put and didn't do anything to start with. She now credits that action with saving her marriage. Based on Susan's advice, Claire chose to forgive her husband's sin and failure, and to seek full reconciliation and healing. Because Susan was willing to share her humiliation and regret, Claire made an informed decision, listening to the advice of someone else who had walked a mile in those awful shoes.

In a world that seeks revenge, is there anything more lovely than forgiveness? After all, we seek it from God every day. We weep over its beauty as we remember the Cross during communion services.

According to Ephesians, God does everything according to the good pleasure of His own will. God loves to forgive, and He does it a lot. Actually, it brings Him pleasure. Heaven rejoices at the forgiveness and repentance of one sinner.

The world in which we live is just the opposite. It's justice, buddy: You made your bed, now you have to sleep in it.

As Christians, we're held to a higher standard—the Word of God. And there is great blessing that follows the command to forgive. I mean, think about it. We serve a mountain-moving God who is more than able to work miracles. And while there should be consequences for sinful behavior between marriage partners, we don't want to take the consequences so far that we cause our mate to lose hope. I'm so thankful that even though Jeff expressed his anger and sadness at my betrayal, he did not hold it over my head, verbally punishing me with constant reminders of my failings.

I understand that it's not always possible for a woman to stay in her marriage. If her husband is unrepentant or unwilling to change his ways, it may be a lost cause. There are times when divorce may be the best course of action—for example, consistent patterns of adultery, ongoing drug abuse, and physical violence.

But those sins are for the most part exceptions. I'm talking about a man who makes a really stupid mistake, or has gotten himself mired in addictive sexual sin but is desperate for a way out. There is a difference.

I don't want to condemn anyone who runs away when betrayal is discovered. But as women, sometimes we give up too quickly in the face of our husband's failures. Negative and hopeless emotions can quickly escalate (especially with the help of well-meaning but slanderous family or girlfriends), and a woman can find herself making rash decisions during the firestorm of unfaithfulness and deception, decisions that she may later regret.

Nothing is too difficult for God. Nothing is impossible for Him. And there is no situation that is beyond His miraculous reach!

Man, He Gets On My Nerves!

Song of Solomon 2:15 says, "Catch for us the foxes, the little foxes that ruin the vineyards, our vineyards that are in bloom." Think of your marriage as a vineyard.

More often than not, it's the little things that wreak havoc upon your relationship—those annoying little personality quirks that seemed cute when you and your husband were first dating. It's important to walk in forgiveness for the everyday irritations that have the potential to *spoil* the companionship, fondness, and romance that should be growing in your marriage. Maybe your husband always runs late—or nags you because *you* always make him late. Or he's a neat freak, and you have three kids in a house that will never be picked up to his standards. Does he talk with his mouth full...interrupt you at dinner parties...keep you awake with his snoring?

Whatever the particular "little foxes" are in your marriage, they need to be met with diligent and persistent acceptance and forgiveness. *Forgiving love* is like a sentry stationed on the watchtower of your vineyard, and is a powerful tool to keep your vineyard blooming, growing, and productive.

5. The Facet of Trusting Love

Like an apple tree among the trees of the forest is my lover among the young men. I delight to sit in his shade. (Song of Solomon 2:3)

My husband is a "shade tree" for me, but it wasn't always so. I used to think I could do everything on my own and that I didn't *really* need him. I didn't want to open myself up to the potential disappointment of desperately needing another person. So, for the first couple of years of our marriage I held myself aloof emotionally, believing that Jesus was all I needed in this life and that I shouldn't put my trust in a mere mortal. Little did I know that I was missing out on one of the greatest blessings that God can give a married woman.

It had started out as a normal flu bug, but due to a nasty relapse I ended up spending over a month on the couch trying to recuperate. And because I was resting so much during the day, I was unable to sleep at night. The doctor prescribed a sleeping pill called Halcion. Grateful, I began taking it right away. This took care of the insomnia, but I remember feeling quite strange during the time I was on that prescription.

My mother informed me soon thereafter that Halcion was a very strong drug, and she suggested I stop taking it so as not to form a dependence on sleeping pills. I had no idea that going off Halcion would create such drama in my life.

After throwing away the remainder of the prescription, I didn't sleep for three nights straight. I don't mean that I didn't get much sleep, or that I was restless. I mean that I did not close my eyes for one minute during those three nights. I sat on the couch curled up in a tight little ball, scared out of my wits. My mind played tricks on me, and my fear in that room was palpable. I became convinced that I would never sleep again—and in my paranoid state nothing could convince me otherwise. My stomach churned, I developed strange ticks, and I lost weight rapidly.

I didn't know at the time that other people had reported similar problems with this drug. (In a *Newsweek* magazine article, some people even claimed to experience amnesia and psychotic episodes.[1]) I just thought I was going crazy!

I found myself desperately seeking comfort—and that's when I turned to Jeff. I stopped trying to handle my problem alone and told him about my deep fears and despondency. Of course he had been aware of the situation, but he had no idea just how bad it had become.

He became my shelter. He became my "shade tree." His strong assurance and loving presence kept me sane during that time. When he discovered that I couldn't sleep, he offered to keep me company by sleeping in the living room, on the pullout couch, with me.

This jolted me from the mind-bending, tormenting insomnia. I no longer felt alone. I savor the sweet memory of Jeff, our son Andrew, and me all snuggled up on the pullout couch together, watching *Anne of Green Gables* for the first time. I took such comfort in the strength of my husband during those dark days.

Jeff called me often from work and took tender care of me while I recuperated. He reminded me of God's love for me. And while I will always be thankful that Jeff rose to the occasion when I needed him most, I have to remember that it was born of my vulnerability. My need and deep distress drove me into the arms of my husband, and I am grateful. Grateful to God for allowing such a horrendous trial, and grateful to Jeff for rising to the occasion when I needed him most!

Becoming vulnerable and trusting your husband may be very difficult for you. Maybe you were hurt as a child or young adult, and you find it hard to trust.

Trusting is hard for everyone. For the most part, we've all been hurt and betrayed at some point in our lives. Don't let excuses rob you of this most intimate treasure of marriage. Trusting is a choice, and with God's help, you can open your heart to your husband's love in a deeper and more profound way.

I feel certain that most husbands would willingly meet their wives' needs if they were given the chance. Unfortunately, we often dismissively convey the "we're fine, thanks" sentiment.

But we're not fine. We were created to deeply need our husbands (and they were created likewise), and we are guilty of holding our men at arm's length.

In this crazy, sometimes frightening world, I encourage you to trust your husband. Pray that God will make him worthy of that trust, then take a leap of faith—and give him a chance to rise to the occasion.

Love Is a Many-Splendored Thing

Society depicts love as changeable, weak, undependable, and disposable. By consuming a steady diet of our current culture's news and entertainment, we run the risk of being convinced that this is truth. For example, Brad Pitt and Angelina Jolie are currently the hottest item out there in Celebrityville. Before that, it was Brad Pitt and Jennifer Aniston; before that, Brad Pitt and Gwyneth Paltrow; and before that...hmmm, well who remembers back that far? I mean, gosh, he's what... forty? Who can blame him for being on his umpteenth "love" affair?

As the hunky movie stars of our day blaze a macho trail through the available young actresses in Hollywood (much like greedy children eating all the chocolates in the box), it would be easy to assume they're living the "good life." But in our topsy-turvy world, we must remember that truth is not relative. Truth does not ebb and flow with the tide of public opinion. The truth about love can be seen in the Word of God and in the behavior of God toward man.

God willing, ten years from now my big Indian husband and I will still be going strong, getting old and wrinkled together, and living out a *real* romance. While pop culture icons trade out marriage partners every few years, the true treasure in life is to nurture and enjoy a lasting marriage relationship. And as we live out a Christian marriage, the real question is, How can we not only reject society's view of love, but also be a beacon of light for what true married love is? In other words, how can we shine brightly in the confused twilight that is *passed off* as real love?

Hopefully as you read this chapter you began to see your husband in the soft light of God's love (and not the glaring, hundred-watt light of criticism and comparison). If so, what have you seen? That he's the same man you fell in love with... the same guy you walked breathlessly down the aisle toward... the man you share your meals, your dreams, your children, and your bed with.

He's *yours*. Maybe his idea of a romantic overture is to take out the trash, gas up the car, or fix the leaky faucet. Well, begin to esteem the average and familiar, because there are plenty of girls out there who would love a husband that serves them in those ways.

I challenge you to *tell him* what he means to you. Why not start today? Why not start right now?

3

The Four Temperaments

ANGELA HOLDS THE AVOCADO-GREEN blender close to her chest while padding softly through the living room. She glances cautiously up the stairs as she passes, making sure Eric is still in the shower. Ever so quietly, she tiptoes through the living room and noiselessly eases the garage door open. Once in the garage she silently lifts the lid of the garbage can and softly sets the thirty-five-year-old "seen better days" blender on top of the trash.

Next, Angela takes old newspapers from a nearby stack, wads them up, and sets them on top of the old blender. On top of the wadded newspapers she adds a cardboard pizza box containing a few crusts from last night's dinner.

There...that should do it.

Later that afternoon, Eric storms into the house.

Eric: *Angela*, why is this perfectly good blender in the trash?!

Angela: Eric, my parents bought us a beautiful new KitchenAid blender for Christmas—we don't need that one.

Eric: What if the new one breaks?

Angela: It won't.

Eric: But this blender is perfectly good—there's nothing wrong with it.

Angela: The glass is cracked, the blades are dull, it's thirty-five years old, and like I said, we have a new blender. And by the way, Eric, why do *you* insist on going through the trash?

Eric: Because you throw away perfectly good stuff!

With that, Eric tucks the antiquated blender under his arm and storms out to the garage, where he will store it in a box labeled Extra Appliances. The box also contains a dented chrome toaster, a Mr. Coffee coffeemaker that's missing its carafe, and a Crock-Pot with faulty wiring that he plans to repair soon.

When Eric and Angela were first dating, she referred to him as "my little pack rat." Now that they are married, she has resorted to sneaking things into the trash can in an effort to clear the house of his ever growing pile of junk. His inclination to "save" everything is no longer cute—but a catalyst for anger and irritation.

We've all heard the saying "opposites attract," but I've found that sometimes "opposites attack." The personality traits and adorable quirks that initially attracted you to your husband can be the very qualities that are now driving you crazy (or in more serious cases, driving you away).

In an effort to study and explain human behavior, Hippocrates came up with the theory of four distinct personality types several thousand years ago. And while this theory is certainly not without flaw, it's a great tool in understanding and appreciating the differences between us. Understanding the different personalities brings validation to traits and temperaments of the people who are *not* like you. With every personality strength there is a weakness. Often in marriage we begin to focus only on the weaknesses. By recognizing and acknowledging that very real differences in our personalities do exist, we can begin to celebrate and appreciate those dissimilarities.

I gained much of my understanding on this topic by reading Tim LaHaye's book *Spirit-Controlled Temperament.* Additionally, the lists of "strengths" below are compiled directly from Florence Littauer's *Personality Plus.*[2] Most people will find that they are a combination of two personality types, with one being dominant. But let's face it, every single person on earth is completely individual and unique. There is no list of traits that will be completely accurate in describing you or me—the lists below are only a rough template. Can you find yourself and your husband somewhere in these lists?

SANGUINE'S PERSONALITY STRENGTHS

Sanguine's Emotions

Appealing personality
Talkative, storyteller
Life of the party
Good sense of humor
Memory for color
Physically holds on to listener
Emotional and demonstrative
Enthusiastic and expressive
Cheerful and bubbling over
Curious
Good on stage
Wide-eyed and innocent
Lives in the present
Changeable disposition
Sincere at heart
Always a child

Sanguine as a Parent

Makes home fun
Is liked by children's friends
Turns disaster into humor
Is the circus master

Sanguine at Work

Volunteers for jobs
Thinks up new activities
Looks great on the surface
Creative and colorful
Has energy and enthusiasm
Starts in a flashy way
Inspires others to join
Charms others to work

Sanguine as a Friend

Makes friends easily
Loves people
Thrives on compliments
Seems exciting
Envied by others
Doesn't hold grudges
Apologizes quickly
Prevents dull moments
Likes spontaneous activities

Melancholy's Personality Strengths

Melancholy's Emotions

Deep and thoughtful
Analytical
Serious and purposeful
Genius prone
Talented and creative
Artistic or musical
Philosophical and poetic
Appreciative of beauty
Sensitive to others
Self-sacrificing
Conscientious
Idealistic

Melancholy at Work

Schedule oriented
Perfectionist, high standards
Detail conscious
Persistent and thorough
Orderly and organized
Neat and tidy
Economical
Sees the problems
Finds creative solutions
Needs to finish what is started
Likes charts, graphs,
figures, lists

Melancholy as a Parent

Sets high standards
Wants everything done right
Keeps home in good order
Picks up after children
Sacrifices own will for others
Encourages scholarship and
talent

Melancholy as a Friend

Makes friends cautiously
Content to stay in background
Avoids causing attention
Faithful and devoted
Will listen to complaints
Can solve others' problems
Deep concern for other people
Moved to tears with
compassion
Seeks ideal mate

CHOLERIC'S PERSONALITY STRENGTHS

Choleric's Emotions

Born leader
Dynamic and active
Compulsive need for change
Must correct wrongs
Strong willed and decisive
Unemotional
Not easily discouraged
Independent and self-sufficient
Exudes confidence
Can run anything

Choleric at Work

Goal oriented
Sees the whole picture
Organizes well
Seeks practical solutions
Moves quickly to action
Delegates work
Insists on production
Makes the goal
Stimulates activity
Thrives on opposition

Choleric as a Parent

Exerts sound leadership
Establishes goals
Motivates family to action
Knows the right answer
Organizes household

Choleric as a Friend

Has little need for friends
Will work for group activity
Will lead and organize
Is usually right
Excels in emergencies

Phlegmatic's Personality Strengths

Phlegmatic's Emotions

Low-key personality
Easygoing and relaxed
Calm, cool, and collected
Patient, well balanced
Consistent life
Quiet but witty
Sympathetic and kind
Keeps emotions hidden
Happily reconciled to life
All-purpose person

Phlegmatic as a Parent

Makes a good parent
Takes time for the children
Is not in a hurry
Can take the good with the bad
Doesn't get upset easily

Phlegmatic at Work

Competent and steady
Peaceful and agreeable
Has administrative ability
Mediates problem
Avoids conflicts
Good under pressure
Finds the easy way

Phlegmatic as a Friend

Easy to get along with
Pleasant and enjoyable
Inoffensive
Good listener
Dry sense of humor
Enjoys watching people
Has many friends
Has compassion and concern

THE MAJOR WEAKNESSES OF THE FOUR PERSONALITY TYPES

Sanguine's Weaknesses

Restless

Weak-willed

Egotistical

Unorganized

No follow-through

Too talkative

Tends to exaggerate

Choleric's Weaknesses

Hot-tempered

Never wrong

Compulsive worker

Impetuous

Self-sufficient

Controlling

Impatient

Melancholy's Weaknesses

Easily depressed

Pessimistic

Moody

Feelings easily hurt

Insecure

Difficult to please

Struggles with unforgiveness

Self-centered

Phlegmatic's Weaknesses

Slow and lazy

Teasing

Selfish and stubborn

Indecisive

Unexcited

Resists change

Procrastinator

Unmotivated

The Trouble with Troubling Relationships:
Validating Opposites

My son, Andrew, and I have had our share of personality clashes during his growing-up years. He was a really good kid to raise, never gave us much trouble, and always picked a great group of kids to hang around with. Our disagreements mostly had to do with the fact that we just didn't see eye to eye on *anything*. I wasn't having arguments with him about staying out too late or coming home with "beer breath"; but his way of thinking was foreign to me, and vice versa. And because Andrew has strong leadership skills (translation: impossible to lead), he was pretty much trying to run the entire household from about the time he was two years old. When someone is described as a "born leader," it's just a nice way of saying they were a bossy toddler.

To be fair, I'm sure the fact that I tend to be a control freak greatly frustrated my born leader—because I was not willing to budge even slightly, nor relinquish even a tiny bit of control. So...we clashed, and clashed, and clashed. My husband, the peacemaker, was the buffer between us.

I'm happy to report that Andrew and I have made it safely through to the other side—finally arriving at a mutually respectful and loving relationship. One of the most helpful factors in our transition from head-butting to appreciation was the day I gained some much-needed insight into the differences between the four personalities.

I was sitting in a seminar given by CLASS Services where the four personalities were being discussed by Marita Littauer, and I had a true "light bulb" moment. I remember hearing the description of the choleric temperament and actually sucking in my breath in astonishment, thinking, *That's Andrew!* To my way of thinking, Andrew was strange because he wasn't like me, and we should all be praying that he would change and become more...more...well, more like *me*. Then he would be normal.

What a tremendous eye-opener it was to realize Andrew was a typical choleric. He didn't need to change and become more like me. Rather, *I* needed to understand why my son acted as he did, and to accept and appreciate him for the person God made him to be. The trouble with our troubling relationship was a lack of understanding, validation, and appreciation.

Let The Sun Shine: Appreciating Opposites

Cut roses are kept in cold storage at floral shops to keep them from blooming. This way, once they are exposed to warmth and a little natural sunlight, they will open with glory. The lovely fragrance fills your home, and the spectacular color of the flowers impresses all who enter.

Acceptance, appreciation, and validation are the warmth that will cause your husband's personality and true self to bloom. Disapproval and disparaging remarks will only shut him down, not change him; worse, they will cause him to retreat from you emotionally.

Men crave respect and must feel valued and important for *who* they are. Valuing the "differences" between you will foster an attitude of gratitude, and help you to refocus on your husband's good points, instead of lingering on your grievances.

Around our house we refer to my husband, Jeff, as "Felix Unger" (the neat one in *The Odd Couple*). Sometimes as I do the dishes I can feel his eyes on my back...watching me. He watches me load the dishwasher and wants to give me a little instruction. He watches me wipe off the counters and would like to give me efficiency tips. He watches me put food scraps down the garbage disposal and can hardly refrain from offering suggestions.

This is Jeff. This is my husband. And I learned long ago to just appreciate who he is and accept that he will have helpful tips and suggestions for every job I do.

Jeff is no longer allowed to watch me pack his lunch. He lost the privilege years ago because of his "tip and suggestion" problem. Most nights after dinner is over, I will pack Jeff's lunch for the next day; he will often sit at the kitchen table while I'm doing this. One night he gave one suggestion too many, sending me over the edge. Dishes didn't go flying, nor did he flee the room in terror—but suffice it to say that I reached the breaking point.

Now, if I catch his eyes wandering over to the counter when I'm packing his lunch, I'll say, "Stop watching me!"—and he quickly averts his eyes. A girl's gotta have boundaries, after all.

But all kidding aside, Jeff's perfectionist Melancholy temperament is who he is. I have learned to deeply appreciate the fact that he likes to vacuum, take out the trash, and generally make things neat. If I don't take myself too seriously, then I can laugh at our differences and value my "Felix" for the stand-up guy he is.

He's Late...Again: Relating to Opposites

"James?" Mary calls down the hall. "Jaaaames, come on, it's time to go!"

James and Mary were supposed to be at the Porters'

dinner party thirty minutes ago, and James is running late again. When Mary walks into the bedroom to hurry James along, she finds him in his socks and underwear, chuckling on his cell phone.

"James—*come on!*"

He finishes his phone call and responds with, "I'm *coming!* Sheeesh, Mary, lighten up!" And yet another evening is off to a rocky start. Another social engagement is marred by ugly feelings and ugly words.

Mary is a stickler for being on time, and James is always running late. When they were dating, it didn't seem like such a big deal—Mary had stars in her eyes, and James was worth waiting for. But now the stars have fallen to earth, and Mary finds James's habitual lateness to be inconsiderate and irritating.

What's the solution?

First and foremost, Mary must recognize that she does not control what James does or when he does it, and that the effort of trying to is making her nuts.

So if Mary does not control James's behavior, whose behavior *does* she control? Only her own. Reaching the conclusion that Mary will never change James is the first step in resolving their conflict.

Second, Mary needs to see her overwhelming sense of irritation at James's lateness as "bait." Satan is a very real enemy who loves to cause division in our marriages. The divorce statistics prove that. The enemy tries to create a wedge between marriage partners, and will often use ridiculous or mundane irritations to do so. What begins as a mild irritant intensifies over time to a full-blown conflict. Mary is being baited into acting ugly toward her husband because she doesn't like, or agree with, his way of doing things.

Third, Mary needs to refocus on what's really important. I

recently read a story about two fathers and their teenage sons who got lost while hiking in the mountains. They had started their twelve-mile hike in perfect weather conditions, but an early winter storm hit them unexpectedly, putting their lives in grave danger. They were finally rescued after four grueling days. The video of the rescue showed them running toward their wives and other children with jubilant smiles and whoops of joy. The four survivors told of the gratitude they felt toward God, that they were given more time on earth to spend with their families. You can bet that the small irritations and annoyances that exist between husband and wife were the last thing on anyone's mind. Why? Because they were reminded of what's really important.

James, the guy sitting on the bed in his socks and underwear...the guy talking on his cell phone as if he hasn't a care in the world...the guy who will probably make Mary late to every party they ever attend. That guy...*he's* what's important. The petty, irritating things he does that displease Mary are not important. James, the man she married, the man she promised to love forever...he's what's important.

What if Mary had walked into the bedroom and, upon finding her adorable husband sitting on the bed talking on his phone in his socks and underwear, smiled, mussed his hair, and given him a kiss on the cheek? And then said pleasantly, "Come on, slowpoke, I'm hoping to taste some of the Porters' famous BBQ ribs tonight"? She might have then walked out of the room, quieted her heart, and reminded herself that she does not control James, and that it will not be the end of the world if they're late...again.

The whole world would continue to turn. Life would go on. And best of all, she would have refused to take the bait, preferring instead to treat her husband with love and respect. They could then have a wonderful evening together, enjoying the party—but more important, enjoying each other.

Understanding and appreciating the fact that we are all wired differently will go a long way in helping us overlook another's shortcomings. There's a pretty good chance that James was not running late to purposely irritate Mary. It's just the way he's always been. Does that mean that James shouldn't be working on his inconsiderate habit of arriving late to social functions? No, not at all. But that's between James and God. Mary should certainly discuss the problem with James and make her wishes known to him—communicating to her husband that showing up late to most functions is irritating and embarrassing. But then she's got to move on, and just work on herself and her own "stuff." The Word of God has something important to say about this:

> Be completely humble and gentle; be patient, bearing with one another in love. (Ephesians 4:2)

Work Together—Not Against Each Other

My friend Candice and her husband, Douglas, are both successful speakers and authors in the health and fitness education field, and are well known throughout their industry. They have been married nearly twenty years, and they learned an important lesson about their personality strengths and weaknesses.

When they first married, they decided to combine their two thriving careers. In the beginning, they continued to do business as usual—each doing *all* the different duties associated with being a fitness consultant. But eventually Douglas and Candice found that this fostered an attitude of competition and criticism. And in an effort to bring unity and camaraderie to their marriage, they decided to divide the workload according to their individual strengths.

Douglas's specialties were negotiating contracts, developing the technical aspects of the programs they were teaching, and conducting the medical and scientific research that supported their findings. Candice, on the other hand, excelled in practical application, and was gifted at presenting techniques in a stimulating, fun, and creative way.

The end result? They found it far more enjoyable and lucrative to work within their particular strengths.

Candice told me that as they began to divide their work accordingly, they no longer felt competitive with each other, because they were now working as a team to build a successful business.

In the early years of their marriage, they adopted 1 Thessalonians 5:11 as their family motto:

Therefore encourage one another and build each other up, just as in fact you are doing.

Accepting and appreciating the differences between you and your husband will go a long way in helping you to build him up. You'll find it easier to pray for your husband in line with *who* God made him to be, and not what *you'd* like him to be. After all, your husband is made in God's image—not yours.

4

Fill Your Cup at Your Own Spring

MY DAUGHTER AMY AND I were shopping recently when an attractive teenager—we'll call her "Katie"—caught our eye (as well as everyone else's). She strutted confidently through the store; hips swinging, hair swishing, shoulders back, bust out, chin lifted high in pretended indifference to those around her. Her snug T-shirt and curve-hugging capris left little to the imagination.

As Katie made her movie-star entrance into the glamorous world of K-Mart, she wondered, *Is everyone looking at me?*

You might say, "How do you know what she was thinking?"

Well, hello—it's because I've *been* Katie. And there's a good chance you have been, too, at some point in your life. To be honest, even at forty-four years old, sometimes I still have to beat back the "Katie" inside me. I'm still in the process of being taught and reminded by the Holy Spirit to find my worth, value, and attractiveness in the passionate love of my husband and not in the admiring glances of other men.

The Bible has something important to say about the exclusivity of our marriage partner, and finding our worth in our *husband's* embrace alone. In Proverbs 5:15–19, we find King

Solomon teaching his son about love and marriage. He uses the apt metaphor of pure, refreshing spring water to signify the private and satisfying lovemaking that should be taking place *only* between marriage partners.

> Drink water from your own cistern, running water from your own well. Should your springs overflow in the streets, your streams of water in the public squares? Let them be yours alone, never to be shared with strangers. May your fountain be blessed, and may you rejoice in the wife of your youth. A loving doe, a graceful deer—may her breasts satisfy you always, may you ever be captivated by her love.

There is something precious and significant that we are giving away when we dress, walk, or act in such a way as to elicit the admiring attention of men other than our husband. Using the Scripture above as a reference, we can learn a couple things about how the Lord designed women.

1. God has put in the heart of every woman a thirst to drink deeply of the attention and affection of her man.
2. God has put in the heart of every woman a desire to captivate her husband's attention.

It's these two desires that the enemy will try to twist and pervert. And it's these two desires we must guard, and then seek to fulfill at home. Let's say I wake up in the morning feeling great; I'm having a good hair day, my skinny jeans fit, and I'm at that "all is well with the world" midpoint in my monthly cycle. The Lord is creating in me a thirst for my husband's attention.

As women, we all know this feeling. God put it in the

heart of a woman to feel sexy, desirable, and attractive—it was His idea. He created within us a thirst for the attention and captivation of our own husbands. He knew that as we sought to fulfill the natural craving for our guy's attention, this would help to create a happy, fulfilled, romantic, and exciting marriage.

But there is a choice to be made here. There are three different ways that we can deal with this God-given "thirst."

Choice #1: Squelch the thirst.

Depending upon how you were raised, or what kind of experiences you went through as a young woman, you may choose to squelch this thirst—deny its right to exist. Or possibly you may be suppressing the need for your husband's affection and attention because of past arguments, unforgiveness, bitterness, or deeply rooted anger.

This very thing happened to my friend Ann recently. She and her husband, Steven, had been married for many years, but they found themselves mired in a deep disagreement that had gone on for several months. The breaking point came one Sunday morning when they asked for prayer after the church service.

As several of us began to seek God in prayer for our dear friends, the Lord showed me that unforgiveness had separated them emotionally as well as physically. When I questioned them about it, they said that as they lay in bed at night they could feel the division that had come between them. The longer they stayed apart physically, the easier it became to stay apart.

They cried, they repented, they forgave each other—and

then they made a choice to come together again. I talked with Ann recently and asked her about that prayer time, and how the ensuing freedom that she and Steven were now experiencing came about.

She said, "You know, Paula, that prayer time at church was a real turning point for us." She told me that she'd like to be able to say that they came home and "boogied all night long," but in reality, it was more of a process. According to Ann, they had to resist the spirit of division that had plagued them for some time; they had to *choose* to come together sexually. Ann had to once again be vulnerable to Steven and stop squelching her physical need for him. She began to once again allow her husband to meet her needs and fulfill her thirst within.

Choice #2: Take your thirst to the mean streets.

> Drink water from your own cistern, running water
> from your own well. Should your springs overflow
> in the streets, your streams of water in the public
> squares? (Proverbs 5:15–16)

Out of habit or appetite, we can make the decision to fulfill our desire for male attention outside the home, seeking the sensual admiring glances of coworkers, the men at our church, or just the average guy on the street. In our culture, it's perfectly acceptable to help yourself to a "heaping helping of male attention." In fact, we are encouraged as women to "flaunt it if you've got it."

But what does God's Word say about how women dress? At this point, you may be tempted to skip over the following Scripture—but wait! Don't skip over God's Word. Read it carefully. I promise, His word is timely. It is appropriate for you today. And it will shed light on every troubling area of our lives as women.

> I also want women to dress modestly, with decency and propriety, not with braided hair or gold or pearls or expensive clothes, but with good deeds, appropriate for women who profess to worship God. (1 Timothy 2:9–10)

The word *modesty* is described as humility, restrained behavior, or lack of self-importance. If I am dressing with modesty, then I am restraining myself from being the bodacious middle-aged woman that I imagine myself to be. And although I'm kind of kidding here, for the most part I'm not. We all have areas that should be restrained.

For example, my friend Janet is wonderfully well-endowed in the bosom arena (no money down...no monthly payment... the real deal, baby). She always takes special care to cover her ample bust and to dress with modesty. Often she will have her husband and/or girlfriends check to see that she is not "giving anything away." And it's important to her that only *her* husband enjoys viewing the beauty that is his alone. Her code name for looking immodest is "Zsa Zsa LaRoo." (Don't ask me—she made it up years ago.) For example, when we're at the mall trying on clothes, Janet will often ask, "Does this make me look too *Zsa Zsa LaRoo*?"

I, on the other hand, don't *ever* have to ask my girlfriends if any cleavage is showing. I would need a push-up bra and a late-stage pregnancy for that to take place! But I do often ask my friends if my jeans are too tight. My sisters and I inherited what we refer to as "the Garner butt" from my mother (Garner was our maiden name). Big, round, and, as my husband likes to say, "shaped like an upside-down heart."

For you younger girls: Believe it or not, big, round fannies were not always in. No—not at all. We big-bottomed girls couldn't find pants to fit...couldn't find underwear to contain all our curvaceous beauty...and were ostracized by the skinny, flat-bottomed girls because of our protruding posteriors. But Jennifer Lopez, Beyonce, and buttock implants have changed all that—although my husband says that men have *always* appreciated curves on their wives! My sisters and I are so excited that our body type is finally "in."

But with the "gift" of a curvy derriere comes the responsibility of covering it modestly and dressing with propriety. The saying "If you've got it, flaunt it" holds no place in the life of a Christian woman. We must make the choice to resist the *pull* of the world, resist the *pull* of our flesh, and resist the *pull* of the enemy to exploit and degrade us.

So, ladies...what should *you* be modestly covering up as you go about your life? I can tell you this—it's likely the part of your body that you're most tempted to *show off*.

Choice #3: Satisfy your thirst for attention and appreciation at home.

Having said that, let me assure you that there is a time and a place *to* show off. But it's behind closed doors. My friend Cassie always goes braless around the house when just she and her husband are at home. He made the request that she do so years before, and ever since then she has made it a point to go *au naturale* when they have a day off together. And before you squirm in your chair, thinking, *I don't see that happening around my house, Paula,* let me say that Cassie is living out the admonition found in this Scripture:

> May your fountain be blessed, and may you rejoice in the wife of your youth. A loving doe, a graceful deer—may her breasts satisfy you always, may you ever be captivated by her love. (Proverbs 5:18–19)

And whether you're cognizant of it or not, you do need your husband to find pleasure in you. You do have a need for affirmation and attention from your man. The question is, are you giving him a chance to show it?

Quit Trying to Catch my Husband's Eye!

My husband and I sat in the outdoor bleachers at a football game a couple of years ago. And while most of the crowd was dressed in multiple layers of cold-weather clothing, the woman in front of us was of the hot-blooded variety. She wore low-rise jeans, a bright red thong, and a belly-baring sweater—all of which would be only *her* business if she weren't sitting directly in front of my husband and me. It was impossible, *absolutely impossible*, to pay attention to the football game with the better part of this woman's bottom coming right out of the top of her jeans. I'm serious when I say I haven't seen that much of another woman's tush since the girl's locker room in high school.

I started off embarrassed for her, thinking, *She must not realize that she's losing her pants—maybe a belt would help.* (I sound like my mother here, don't I?) I moved on from embarrassed to puzzled: *Come on, it's cold out here—she must know*

that she's mooning all the people in the row above her. Finally
I settled on angry. *Okay, Sugar Bunny, I'm on to you. You're
short on your daily quota of "Do men notice me? Am I pretty?"
and you're trying to get it from my husband!*

The worst part is that I've done the same thing. Maybe not
with a bright red thong (okay, definitely not with a bright red
thong), but in other, more subtle ways.

However, I'm maturing in my role as a Christian woman.
I've been allowing the Holy Spirit to deal with me, correct me,
and refine me—and I am growing. We *should* be growing up
in Christ, leaving the foolish and childish ways behind us. As
we seek to raise godly daughters, let's do our best to set a godly
example for them to follow.

Women know other women. I'm sure you'd agree that
we pretty much see each other's tricks coming three miles
away. Sometimes an attractive woman will assume that other
women are jealous of her because they seem standoffish. But
very often, that's just not the case. Ladies can be standoffish
when they perceive that a woman is seeking the attention of
all the men in the room.

There's a scene in the movie *Runaway Bride* with Julia
Roberts that illustrates this. In it, Maggie, the character played
by Julia Roberts, is standing by home plate watching a small-
town baseball game in which her best friend's husband, Cory,
is playing.

When Cory steals third base Maggie goes crazy, jump-
ing up and down, shirt flying...hair flying...she's unabashed
in her enthusiasm as she shouts, "Excellent! Excellent!" from
the sidelines.

The next batter hits a base hit, giving Cory a chance to
slide into home, making it by the smallest of margins. As he
comes off the field Maggie is there to meet him, lavishing Cory
with exuberant praise, hugs, and high fives.

Later, Maggie apologizes to her best friend for going over-board in her complimentary behavior toward Cory, telling her that she doesn't mean to flirt with him. Cory's wife responds, "I know. I think sometimes you just sort of spaz out with excess flir-tatious energy, and it just lands on anything male that moves."

Every time I see that scene, I laugh and think of my high school days. My mother pronounced me boy crazy and kindly used that as the excuse for my ho-hum grades during my last few years of high school. As a married woman, I choose to take my flirtatious energy and turn it toward my handsome husband.

Filling your cup at another man's sink leaves you in a pre-carious position—as I found out when I sought the attention of the pastor years ago. In reality, I was playing with fire, put-ting my entire family in danger—as well as myself.

Danger Ahead

Sue sits on her couch comfortably watching *Wheel of Fortune*. A cozy patchwork quilt covers her legs as she cradles a steam-ing cup of hot tea. Lifting the cup gingerly to her lips, she blows gently on the tea and takes a sip.

Then…a faintly smoky smell floats by her nose. She sniffs at the air. Yes…it's definitely smoke she smells. When she slowly turns her head to look, she sees black smoke billowing out of the kitchen.

Sue giggles at something funny on the TV show while flames engulf the kitchen and spread to the living room, ignit-ing the drapes. Sue sips her tea contentedly. Her six-year-old daughter Annie, unaware of the imminent danger, plays quietly in her room down the hall.

What would you say to Sue if you were to drive by her house at that moment? You'd scream and pound on the front door, trying to get her attention. You might yell, "Sue, grab your daughter NOW and get out of that burning house!"

I was the woman in the burning house, and it was my precious family that I put in danger by not being aware. And having counseled women who are dabbling in flirtatious and/ or adulterous relationships, I know that it can be like trying to talk a stubborn four-year-old out of the swimming pool on a hot summer day. Although they don't want to suffer the consequences of disobedience, there is just something so darn refreshing and delicious about staying in the pool.

I have sat across from women over coffee and literally begged them to come out of sin. I have given them specific directions on how to get out before it's too late. I have prayed with them. I have cried with them. And in some cases, I have rejoiced with them as they ran from the burning building.

Run, Baby, Run!

As you examine your heart, do you see yourself in this chapter? Can you recall times when you sought the affirmation and attention from a man other than your husband? If so, let me offer you some words of instruction and encouragement. The following are two things I wish I had done at the beginning of my flirtatious affair with the pastor.

#1: Be transparent and honest with your husband.

A preteen girl from our church recently asked me if I thought kissing a boy was a sin. I told her that was between her and

God, but that a good indicator of sin was anything you had to hide. I used the example that if she was a newlywed and I walked into a room while she was kissing her new husband— would she be embarrassed or run away? She laughed and said, "Of course not!" I then compared it to kissing a boy in her classroom while nobody else was around. If I walked into the classroom during that kiss, what would she do? She said, "Oh, I would run and hide!"

When people become secretive, something's up.

Same thing in marriage. When you find yourself getting secretive, you need to examine your motives. God gave you your husband for your protection. Men understand other men, and know how they operate, just like women know how other women operate. If I had been completely honest with my husband about the amount of time I was spending with the pastor, he would have immediately vocalized his displeasure.

Husbands want to protect their wives and be chivalrous, but we need to give them the opportunity to do so by being honest with them about all male relationships in our lives— work, church, neighborhood, online, etc.

Speaking of online integrity and transparency: If your husband were to read *all* of your e-mails, or instant messaging, or text messages, how would he react? Is your communication with men completely aboveboard? Let's say your husband decides to take a look at your private e-mail account. If he reads anything in there that would cause you to feel embarrassed or defensive, then you have a problem.

Perhaps you felt instantly convicted when I mentioned e-mail correspondence. Maybe what began as a platonic online "friendship" has slowly become a fun, flirtatious, almost romantic relationship. And although you love your husband, this ongoing e-mail exchange is starting to thrill you. If you answer yes to one or more of the questions below, then you're drinking from the wrong watering hole.

1. Do you check your e-mail compulsively, hoping to see *his* name in the inbox?
2. Do you often laugh out loud at his clever comments... blush when he throws a little flattery your way...sigh with contentment when he shares his emotions with you?
3. Have you ever gotten up at night to check your e-mail and correspond with this man?
4. Do you glance around to make sure no one is watching while you read e-mails from him?

Out of the (In)Box and into the Bed

Lynn started off her friendship with Bill in a chat room. As a committed Christian, wife, and mother of three, Lynn had no intention of getting mired in an ungodly, sinful relationship. She was simply curious and bored.

Bill and Lynn hit it off right away. His clever little comebacks, obvious intelligence, and talent for deep and meaningful communication impressed Lynn and kept her coming back for more.

Over time they decided to exchange photos, which only fueled the fire of intimacy, and eventually bumped up the level of sexual innuendo expressed in their secret e-mails. As they grew closer, it became apparent to them both that they should meet.

A terrible fight with her husband, Anthony, gave Lynn the excuse she needed to set up a face-to-face with Bill. And while Lynn was disappointed to discover that Bill wasn't all she had hoped, their relationship continued, finally resulting in adultery.

Because of the constant guilt that Lynn felt, she eventually separated from Anthony. And now that the forbidden fruit had been sampled and was no longer forbidden—well, Bill was out of the picture also.

The turning point came when a hotel room receipt with Bill's name on it showed up in the mail, causing Anthony to suspect that Lynn was involved with someone else. When confronted by Anthony, Lynn admitted everything. Then she repented deeply from her heart and asked for her husband's forgiveness.

Anthony forgave, and God restored. It was a long process, and Lynn admits that her actions hurt her husband deeply. The funny part was that if the hotel receipt hadn't come to the house, Lynn would never have confessed to the adultery. And by her own admission, if she hadn't confessed to the adultery, she doubts the marriage would have survived. It was only in exposure, followed by honesty and transparency, that God's restorative power could begin its work. Once the truth was out in the open, the rebuilding process began.

Six years later, Anthony and Lynn's marriage is solid. Lynn is grateful that she didn't leave Anthony for Bill, "the charming impostor." She told me recently, "Anthony may not shower me with compliments or lavish me with praise, but he shows love to me in a million little ways." These include his hard work, diligence with their finances, small delightful surprises, and his loving way with their children.

In the end, Lynn discovered what so many of us now know—that the man she always wanted really was the one she already had.

#2: Recognize and kill the monster of self-obsession.

My son, Andrew, had trouble with ear infections as a little boy. I remember many instances of his calling for me in the middle of the night, and finding him burning up with a 105-degree fever. I would fill the bath with tepid water and begin the process of trying to cool him down.

The problem was not his fever; it was the ear infection causing a fever. In other words, the fever was only a symptom of Andrew's true medical condition. The fever helped us to know there was a problem that needed our attention.

In much the same way, the self-obsession I felt during my too-close friendship with the pastor was an indicator of the internal war waging in my heart and mind.

Here are a few behaviors that might indicate that your "self-obsession" indicator light is on:

1. You have become the main character in every scene of your life: "How do I feel? Am I truly happy? Is my husband meeting my needs?"
2. You find yourself almost obsessed by your clothing choices each morning.
3. There is more money in the plastic surgery fund than in the college fund.
4. The attention of the new guy at work has motivated you to begin dieting and exercising to lose weight.
5. You are spending more time smiling in front of the mirror than smiling at your husband.
6. You find that your children have suddenly taken a backseat in your daily thoughts and activities.
7. You find it easier and easier to rationalize half-truths when explaining your actions to your husband.

If you fit two or more of these behaviors, be honest with yourself. Call it what it is, and deal with it. Here are some helpful tools that will act as the aspirin to the fever of self-obsession.

1. Return to your first love—Christ. The foundation for a happy life is a close, prayerful, and intimate relationship with Jesus Christ. This relationship takes maintenance and diligence in order to continue growing and remain relevant in our lives.

When I began to satisfy my thirst for attention from the pastor, I was slowly diverting my attention—first from Christ, and then from my husband.

I encourage you to return to your first love as never before. Do the things you did at first: carve out quality time with God each day, read His Word each day, spend time praying, attend church regularly. Simple things, really...but they seem to be the first ones to go when our lives begin to derail.

2. Return to your covenant love—your husband.

Make the choice to turn your heart toward your man. At the same time, resist the urge to have your "love cup" filled up by other men's attention or desire.

Deliberately put your focus back on your husband—the man you would have followed to the moon *before* the wedding. Turn your heart, your mind, and most important, your body in the direction of your husband. This is a surefire way to bring down the fever of self-obsession.

3. Bring more accountability into your life. The best way to eradicate dysfunctional and destructive behavior is to bring it out in the open. Remember, it's only as issues are brought into God's light that healing can come. If you have admitted to "drinking from the wrong spring," then this is the time to share your struggle with others. Find a trusted older woman in your church whom you can confide in, or ask your pastor and his wife for counsel.

4. Clean out the closet. There have been times in my life when I felt strongly convicted to get rid of certain articles of clothing in my closet. If we are sensitive to the leading of the Holy Spirit in our lives, then He has free reign to convict us, refine us, and grow us up.

My sisters and I attended Catholic school for most of our growing up years, and we wore uniforms to school. A constant battle between the nuns and the teenage girls at our school was the required length of the plaid skirts. The nuns would occasionally have all of us kneel on the ground for a "skirt check." They would take out a ruler and measure the inches from the ground to the top of the skirt. The rule was it could be no more than three inches above the knee. This was one test I *never* passed! We Garner girls had long legs—and we were growing fast. Could I help it that my skirt was eight inches from my knee? I'm telling you, I was completely innocent!

Okay...the truth was, I was wearing last year's skirt (one of the benefits of being a teenage beanpole). The new skirt my mom had purchased for me was safely tucked away on the top shelf of my closet—to be worn next year (see how brilliant a fifteen-year-old can be?). To be completely honest, I liked the attention a short skirt provoked. Since this was not an all-girl's Catholic school, I don't need to explain *why*. Even in high school, I was building an appetite for what I call "sexy attention." And before I gave my life fully to God, my appetite flourished.

There was a time in my early twenties, shortly after I gave my heart to the Lord, when I reluctantly threw out all my excessively short skirts and dresses. And to be honest, I wasn't singing "I Surrender All" as I tossed some of my cutest clothes in the trash can. It was hard! I had enjoyed showing off my long legs.

I was surprised to find how much of my identity as a woman was tied up in what I looked like—not in who I was on the inside. But as a young married woman, the Lord was teaching me to find my identity in two things: first in Christ, as a pure daughter of the King of kings; and second, as Jeff Friedrichsen's wife.

5. Flee the wrong relationships. There are important and determined steps you can take to sever wrong relationships in your life. Let's take a look at what God's Word has to say about the subject:

> Flee from sexual immorality. All other sins a man commits are outside his body, but he who sins sexually sins against his own body. Do you not know that your body is a temple of the Holy Spirit, who is in you, whom you have received from God? You are not your own; you were bought at a price. Therefore honor God with your body. (1 Corinthians 6:18–20)

According to *Roget's Thesaurus*, the word *flee* means "to escape from; run away from; hasten from, take flight." When I looked up the word *flee* in *Strong's Exhaustive Concordance of the Bible*, I discovered that the original Hebrew meaning was "clean or pure."

In other words, escaping sexual temptation means remaining pure—or returning to purity, if you've already blown it. So how do you escape? Well, I'm about to give you several suggestions. But if you're involved in a less-than-savory male "friendship," you're not going to like them. Everything in you is going to say, "That's just too drastic. I don't need to go *that* far! I've pretty much got this thing under control. I've heard what

Paula is saying—I agree—and that's enough. I can handle it."

Beware of that attitude. If you react strongly to the next few suggestions, then you most likely need to take them to heart.

A. If the "friendship" has been consummated through e-mail, change your e-mail account immediately.

There is no excuse for not doing this. It will be worth the time-consuming process of giving out your new e-mail address to those who need it. Creating a new account and discontinuing the old ensures that at least this form of communication is cut off.

B. Change your cell phone number and discontinue the "text messaging" option.

You may say, "I can screen my calls." Yeah, well…you could—but you won't. We all think we're stronger than we really are. Why not completely remove the temptation?

C. If the man works in the same office as you, consider changing jobs.

D. If need be, change churches.

Flirtatious relationships often start in a church environment. Just think about it: First off, we have a very real enemy—the devil. He is looking for ways to bring disrepute upon the body of Christ and to slip unnoticed into brother/sister Christian relationships. In addition to this, we usually esteem the

Christians that we work closely with. In hindsight, I can see that one of the reasons I sought the attention of the pastor was because I esteemed his gifts and callings.

How many times have we heard about the choir director and the pianist running off together? It's not because they were just wicked, wicked people, and boy are we glad that they were "found out" so that our church can now move on without spot or blemish. No, it's just people acting like people. If you work closely with a person of the opposite sex (especially if you spend a lot of time alone together), then there is a possibility that you will find yourself attracted to them.

Killing the monster of "self-obsession" is being willing to make a fresh start in a new church community. You would be doing this for three reasons: first, for the sake of your husband; second, for the sake of the other man that you find yourself attracted to (and his family, if he has one); and third, for yourself.

Putting others first may require that you be completely honest with your husband and tell him about the attraction so that he understands your need to change churches. But don't worry; he can take it. You may think he'll just be too hurt or disappointed to know that you felt (or possibly acted on) an attraction to another man—but in the end, I believe it will bring health to your marriage, ultimately helping you relish and enjoy the husband God gave you.

Ladies, I propose that we do our best to raise the bar on our behavior when it comes to seeking the attention, desire, and favor of men other than our husbands. I challenge you to save your best smiles for Mr. Right, your most flirtatious giggles for the guy who gave you the ring, and those super-low-cut stretch jeans for the one who has the right to peel them off you.

5

Who Keeps the Gate Key?

You are a garden locked up, my sister, my bride; you are a spring enclosed, a sealed fountain. (Song of Solomon 4:12)

THESE ARE THE ROMANTIC, poetic words spoken by King Solomon to his bride, the Shulamite maiden. She responds to his amorous overture with this:

Awake, north wind, and come, south wind! Blow on my garden, that its fragrance may spread abroad. Let my lover come into his garden and taste its choice fruits. (Song of Solomon 4:16)

And like any red-blooded Israelite male, Solomon takes her up on her offer:

I have come into my garden, my sister, my bride; I have gathered my myrrh with my spice. I have eaten my honeycomb and my honey; I have drunk my wine and my milk. (Song of Solomon 5:1)

Wow! That's some pretty passionate Scripture! Don't you just love that sex and marriage were God's idea? Not only was it His idea that we procreate in the act of sex, but it was intended for our pleasure as well.

The metaphor of a "private garden" used in this piece of Scripture perfectly illustrates the refreshment, enchantment, and pleasure that lovemaking can bestow upon the participants. The "work" involved in tending a garden is well worth the effort because it awards the recipients with a bounty of life-giving sustenance. A garden provides a place of beauty and reprieve for the soul. Yes, it needs attention—but it also furnishes shade in the heat of day and a private place to rest in the midst of a busy productive life. A garden is a place to linger...a place to relish the loveliness that surrounds...a place to meander and dawdle, to enjoy delectable fruit, and to revel in the beauty of the flowers. You don't run madly through a garden; you walk slowly, listening, watching, and admiring. A well-tended garden will yield a variety of different colors, textures, smells, and tastes. With regular weeding, occasional pruning, skilled tilling, and plenty of water, your garden will explode with fruitfulness, brightness, and abundance. But if you've ever seen a neglected garden, it is dry and unproductive—a sad sight, really, because of all its wasted potential.

Our sex lives are a garden of refreshment given to us by a loving Creator—an important part of life, meant to receive attention and appreciation. Lovemaking is not just another *job*, as in, "Well, I guess it's time to go pick strawberries again." Instead, we should anticipate lovemaking as the blessing it is: "Hey! We *get* to pick strawberries again!"

Think of this chapter as a refresher course on "The Joy of Gardening." Because we all know that you greatly enjoyed "gardening" when you were first married to your husband. In fact, some of you wanted to *garden* every night. It could be that your garden just needs a little TLC. With the "water" of your attention, the "tilling" of communication, the "weeding" of forgiveness, and the "pruning" of selflessness, your garden can bloom with passion once again. So, grab your pruning shears and watering can, and let's get busy.

Who Is This Guy You Married?

This book is about returning to your first love and your covenant love. It is an encouragement to run upon the fragrant path of remembrance, recalling with affection all the reasons you first fell in love with your husband. It is a journey, of sorts, into your past—with the hope that as you gather a perfumed bouquet of sweet memories, you will proceed into a future of delighting in your husband, of opening the garden gate wide for him.

So...why did you first fall in love with *him*? Let's take a minute or two and bring to mind how this whole thing got started. For me, it was Jeff's killer smile. His smile made me swoon and caused my head to spin—and he wasn't even smiling at me!

Jeff owned a furniture store right next door to the bank where I worked, and each day his girlfriend, Gail, would pop by to say hello. I remember watching his face light up as he greeted her, thinking he had the most beautiful smile I had ever seen. To make a long story short, he and Gail eventually broke up, and soon he was giving *me* that gorgeous smile.

I fell in love with all the seemingly insignificant things about my husband: his hands, his laugh, his stories, his wisdom, his patience, his kindness, and his chivalry.

What about you? What are some of the attributes and

qualities that caught your eye when you first met your husband? Do you remember how you felt on those first few dates...how your heart would race when he called you...and how you couldn't stop smiling during those first few months? All those wonderful traits are still there—waiting to be appreciated, recognized, and enjoyed.

Does He Have a Key?

> The husband should fulfill his marital duty to his wife, and likewise the wife to her husband. The wife's body does not belong to her alone but also to her husband. In the same way, the husband's body does not belong to him alone but also to his wife. Do not deprive each other. (1 Corinthians 7:3–5)

To fully understand a particular Scripture, we sometimes need to examine it alongside another Scripture. It's true that the "wife's body does not belong to her alone but also to her husband." But when you read that verse by the romantic candlelight of the Song of Solomon, it makes more sense—it becomes a thing of beauty and excitement.

My body does not belong to me alone—it is my husband's also. And based upon Song of Solomon 4:12, I am his private *garden* of delights...I am a restricted *fountain* (no access allowed without the key), sparkling with the promise of enjoyment...I am an *enclosed spring*, offering refreshment to him alone, and hidden from view.

In Song of Solomon we see the wife inviting her husband into the garden, totally unrestrained and abandoned. She loves him, she trusts him, and she gives herself to him—without a long list of rules. She's not overly concerned with what's about to happen—she simply says, "Come into my garden and taste its choice fruits."

Many times we spend a lot of energy slapping our husband's hands off the fruit tree—instead of inviting him in to have a look around. As women, we can be guilty of assuming dictatorial ownership of the garden. "Umm, not tonight. I have allergies...a headache...a big day tomorrow." It's easy for us to get hung up on having our own needs met, or to become a "Dottie Do-Gooder" (never saying no to anyone's request for help), instead of meeting our husband's needs.

Kudos to you if you're the first one to cook meals for the infirm, head up the nursery program at church, or donate your time to the local orphanage. But keep in mind that your greatest ministry is as a *wife* (yes, even before motherhood).

Just as you consider it a priority to clothe your kids or provide dinner for your husband, so should you prioritize your husband's sexual needs.

Of course, there are exceptions to this rule: a husband who is not interested in having sex with his wife, or a husband whose failings (a wife beater, substance abuser, compulsive adulterer, etc.) make it impossible to connect with him in this way. Those issues are incredibly important, and worthy of discussion—but they are issues that time and space will not allow me to cover in this book. For those of you who find yourselves in situations such as those listed above, I have included several helpful resources at the conclusion of this chapter.

I am talking about your normal, average man who would absolutely *love* for his wife to be more interested in having sex. The guy who wants his wife to loosen up in the bedroom—throw out the list of do's and don'ts and have some fun...the man who doesn't want to have to beg and plead to be let into *his* garden—but instead is invited in. Being invited in means that he is *wanted*.

In addition to his needs, *we* need the physical comfort and sexual pleasure that our husbands offer. Some of you might say, "No, actually, I *don't* need my husband sexually." I respectfully disagree. I would suggest that you feel this way because you have let your appetite for sexual fun and connection wane—and now you don't believe that you are in need of your husband's "sexy attention."

> Awake, north wind, and come, south wind! Blow on
> my garden, that its fragrance may spread abroad. Let
> my lover come into his garden and taste its choice
> fruits. (Song of Solomon 4:16)

When I think about the maiden calling upon the wind to come and blow upon her garden, I think about the word *enticement*. She's enticing her husband with her feminine charms. She's like my friend Cassie whom I spoke about earlier, going braless around the house at her husband's request. Cassie was enticing her husband. She was in essence saying, "Hey, buddy, take a look at these!"

How long has it been since you showed off *your* stuff? Okay...how long since you haven't changed into your pajamas in the bathroom or the closet? We women can be shy when it comes to our bodies—but husbands love to see their wives naked (a lovemaking quagmire). Here are a few suggestions and solutions to the most common problems and setbacks to letting loose in the "garden."

Husbands generally love to have sex with the lights on, but women can be insecure about being seen completely naked. A great solution is to have one lamp in your bedroom with a dim lightbulb for the purpose of creating some "soft light." Or light some candles to give the room a romantic glow. Guys are visual, and the lovemaking experience is far more pleasurable for them if they can see what's going on. Remember, your husband loves you. He isn't focused on your physical flaws, like stretch marks or cellulite—he's interested in the main attraction. He isn't looking for perfection; his desire is for warmth, availability, and interest.

Is your tummy too big, hips kind of lumpy, booty a bit droopy? Well, camouflage, baby! There are many ways to artfully present your best assets, and still delight your husband by the sight of your body. Use your imagination, take a long look at the "intimates" section at the department store, and be daring.

We all go through difficult stages in our lives when things are especially hectic: raising small children, working full-time, or the stress of taking care of aging parents. Because of this, you may feel too tired at night to really enjoy lovemaking. Some solutions to this problem may be to: invite your husband home for lunch and "serve" yourself; ask a good friend to take your kids for an hour at dinnertime, while you're still fresh; or get a lock on your bedroom door and put the kids to bed early.

The point is not the *when*, *where*, and *how* of lovemaking, but rather that you carve out time for it no matter what's going on in your life.

The way one woman invites and entices her husband may be completely different from the next woman. Even though I probably don't sound very shy and demure to you, in many ways I am. I might not be even remotely comfortable doing some of the crazy or exotic things you are willing to do to entice your husband. Thankfully, I'm only responsible to be the best Paula I know how to be—and by doing so, I am sure to bless my husband.

No Access Allowed

Joan and I discussed her marriage over dinner at a local restaurant. She and Nicholas had been married for fifteen years and their sex life was almost completely nonexistent. Since having her three children, Joan had put on close to seventy-five pounds. She was disappointed with herself and felt unattractive. The longer she put off Nicholas, the harder it became to give herself to him. It was beginning to feel unnatural to have sex with her husband because their encounters were so few and far between.

Joan admitted to never changing her clothes in front of Nicholas. Her reasons were twofold: She felt chubby, and she didn't want to turn him on by letting him see her naked (talk about a dichotomy).

Most of us have been guilty of wanting to deny our husbands access to the garden because we're afraid we don't look good enough. First off, let's agree that it's easier to feel sexy when you're fit and trim. That's really a no-brainer. But since real life dictates that we generally gain weight as we age, pregnancy may have left us with a few battle scars, and the force of gravity is steadily pulling down those body parts we don't want pulled down—well, we are going to have to choose to get over ourselves.

Just as I don't expect my husband to stay in the exact same physical shape he was in when I married him, he doesn't labor under the misconception that I will remain twenty-two forever.

Having said that, I want to stress that it's important to do our best to stay attractive for our husbands. If you desire to give yourself unreservedly in lovemaking, it will be a whole lot easier if you're within a normal size range for your body type. For most of us, "normal" is going to be a lot different from what's represented in culture these days. Some women are just naturally rounder than others, for example. Maybe you're top heavy, or bottom heavy, or tummy heavy. Do your best to stay healthy and fit, and then accept yourself—I can almost guarantee that your husband does.

Joan had two choices to make. First she could accept herself as she was and realize that the reason Nicholas always wanted to "catch" her changing was because the sight of her naked still excited him (thank God for that!). Second, she could make sure that she was eating right and exercising. She was not without choices. In fact, at that point in their marriage she was holding all the cards when it came to their sex life. Nicholas was a willing and eager partner. The ball was in her court, and she could make the changes necessary to let the breath of God once again stir up the sexual embers.

This Garden Gate Is Locked

Another major deterrent to giving a husband the key to the garden gate is a past that involves sexual molestation.

Some women are in bondage when it comes to sex. I don't mean that they need to "loosen up" a little and learn to have some fun. No, it's far more serious than that; they are actually in bondage to something that happened to them as girls or young women. Sexual abuse can scar a woman's mind and heart, making her unable to give herself fully to her husband. She may feel almost violated by him each time they have sex. Although her mind *knows* that her husband has every right to want intimacy from her, her heart tells her she's being violated. She may even think, *I can't believe he wants this from me! Doesn't he know how this makes me feel?*

Being violated as a child (or young adult) sets up a woman to feel out of control the rest of her life in the area of sex. The admonition in Scripture that "a woman's body is not her own" repels her—makes her feel like a "piece of meat" instead of a valued human being. The abused woman misunderstands God's design for sex, and will often only acquiesce to physical unity out of a source of duty—or simply to keep the peace in her home. She has missed the unique beauty and physical thrills of sex, and sees only the ugliness of being taken advantage of.

If I have just described you, my precious friend, my heart hurts that you had to go through sexual abuse—but there is healing. True, lasting, deep, abiding healing. A healing so real that nothing can ever take it from you. A healing that is so radical that you will be able to open wide the gate, invite your husband in, and have the time of your life.

From Darkness to Light

Kimberly, a dear friend of mine, was married in her early twenties to a solid, kind-hearted guy named Ron. They lived together for a couple of years before they were married, and their sex life was wonderful and plentiful. But almost from the time that they wed, Kimberly found herself uninterested and almost repulsed by sex.

What happened? Where were the fireworks…the magic…the fun?

After a year of marriage, Kimberly and Ron gave their hearts to the Lord and began the journey that would define the rest of their lives. And while becoming a Christian brought tremendous changes into Kim's life, her attitude about sex remained unchanged. As time progressed, Kimberly began to have flashbacks to a time when a close family relative had sexually molested her in her childhood. She would do her best to block out the images, only to have them crop up again and again. Although the abuse had been a conscious memory all along, her new marriage seemed to have pushed the memories to the forefront of her mind.

Kim cried out to God in prayer over the increasing darkness that she was experiencing, and He answered her prayer in a dramatic and wonderful way. She went to hear a special speaker at her church one night who talked about sexual abuse and the resulting bondage that can come from it. Hope rose in Kimberly's heart as she made her way down the aisle for prayer. And as those who gathered around her to pray cried out to God on her behalf, the bondage broke! It was sudden, dramatic, and real. The flashbacks stopped completely, the revulsion to sex disappeared, and forgiveness for her molester came. Ron noticed the change in her immediately, and they both recognized that God had done a supernatural work.

Many go through a healing process that transpires much more slowly. But the point is not the speed at which God heals; rather, it is the fact that God does indeed heal! Whether God's healing comes quickly or progressively through counseling, prayer, and patience, the result is the same—freedom! Freedom to forgive, freedom to forget, and freedom to enjoy lovemaking the way the Lord intended.

I don't want to belabor this point, since this book is not about sexual abuse. But since many women have been molested as children in one degree or another, I feel it is a topic worth broaching—especially since this kind of abuse can greatly affect sexual intimacy. After all, it's difficult to unabashedly open the garden gate in a revealing negligee if you feel as though you're being molested all over again every time you have sex.

If you've been reading this chapter and thinking, *She's*

telling my story, then you must take the bondage to God. He doesn't play favorites—what He did for Kimberly, and so many others like her, He will also do for you. He is well able to do it, and is looking for faith no bigger than a mustard seed. Stretch out your hand to Him today, right now, and ask Him to heal you. He will. He is good and faithful.

> Praise the LORD, O my soul, and forget not all his benefits—who forgives all your sins and heals all your diseases, who redeems your life from the pit and crowns you with love and compassion, who satisfies your desires with good things so that your youth is renewed like the eagle's. The LORD works righteousness and justice for all the oppressed. (Psalm 103:2–6)

It's All About Appetite

Food. So much of what we want in life is based upon *appetite.* For example, by choosing to eat lots of fruits, vegetables, and whole grains, I am building an appetite for good food. My healthy lifestyle is not the by-product of a long list of no's—like no Doritos, no hot dogs, and no chocolate milk. I have a healthy lifestyle because I have built up an *appetite* for nutritious food like steamed broccoli and fresh fruit.

    Church. I regularly attend church, and I find that I miss it when I can't go. Over time, an *appetite* has been built for the stability, growth, and love that my local church offers me. I am now hooked on my church.

    Exercise. I love to walk. Taking long walks is one of my favorite things to do. It gives me time to think and pray. I like to walk alone because it has developed into an important prayer time for me. When time allows, I sometimes walk for up to two hours, just taking in the scenery and enjoying the fresh air. I have developed an *appetite* for walking.

Sex. By regularly engaging in an expressive, open, and un-restrained sex life, I am building an *appetite* for more of the same. The more I say yes, the more I want to say yes. Every time I make the effort to wear something cute and suggestive around him, wink at him over the top of the kids' heads at the dinner table, or send him a provocative and promising e-mail, I am building an appetite for sex with my husband.

A Real Man Is Better Than an Airbrushed Fantasy

I talked in an earlier chapter about the temptation to be af-firmed through admiring, sexually charged looks from other men. We discussed the need to resist creating an appetite for the illicit and instead allowing our husbands to fulfill that need. But there are other counterfeit ways in which women can fill the need for the love and attention that only their husbands should be giving them.

Maybe your man has fallen *way* short of what you think a husband should be. Is he grumpy, loud, boring, smelly, short-tempered, never talks, or never shuts up? Whatever your complaints, I'm not minimizing them or telling you they don't really exist. But you know what? You've got your own annoy-ing stuff, too. We all do.

One of the greatest provokers of marital dissatisfaction is comparison. If you're in the habit of comparing your husband to other men, you will find it difficult to grant him unrestricted access to your "garden of delights." And whether you're comparing him to a man at church, your best friend's husband, your boss at work, or Denzel Washington, the very act of comparison will set your standards impossibly high, leaving your husband out in the cold.

The pitfall of "comparison" affects men as well as women. Just like we as women can't possibly measure up to the airbrushed images found in the Victoria Secret catalog, our husbands can't measure up to the airbrushed images found in romance novels, soap operas, movies, or TV sitcoms.

I told you earlier about Lynn, who started an online relationship with Bill through e-mail. Bill did an excellent job of "airbrushing" himself for Lynn. He said only what was well thought-out and intelligent—I'm sure the spellchecker came in handy for that—and sent just the right photo of himself to her. She told me how surprised she was to find that he was much shorter than he had led her to believe. (Wow, macho online wife-stealer turns out to be a liar—big surprise!)

But if any of us are given a choice, we usually do "airbrush" ourselves to create something better then we really are. My latest set of ministry photos was taken with a special filter on the lens of the camera. When my photographer, Michael, first told me he wanted to use it this time around, I said, "But Mike, we've never used a filter before." He tactfully suggested that at my age, the filter would only enhance the pictures. And guess what? They were the best set of pictures ever! I actually looked *younger* in them than in the previous set, taken in my thirties. Yeah…I'll never go anywhere without a filter again!

Romance novels, romantic chick flicks, and the like do the same thing for men. A guy in a romance novel has been airbrushed through the intellect and imagination of the (usually) female author. Of course he's going to look great! If I sat down to write dialogue for my husband, he would say things like,

"Oh Paula, baby, *darling*, you're the wind beneath my wings. My precious kitten, your smile lights up my world!" But then it wouldn't be Jeff talking, would it? (Or any other man I know, for that matter.) It would be an airbrushed, emasculated version of the "real" man I call my husband.

It's not our job to give our husbands an extreme personality makeover—it's our job to respect them consistently, love them deeply, and pray for them constantly.

Think about it this way: When we're diligently looking for a guy to spend the rest of our lives with, we're attracted to someone like the Marlboro Man—strong, silent, and rugged. But we've hardly taken off the wedding gown before we're trying to make him over into Fabio—sensitive, touchy-feely, and poetic.

As women, we are sometimes guilty of inadvertently building an appetite for "hearts and flowers" through the consumption of fictional romance—an appetite that our husbands may simply be unable to fill. Once the appetite for such fare has been developed, it's easy to pull out the magnifying glass of comparison and say, "How come *you* never plan any romantic getaways to Europe?" or "Can't *you* be the one to get a babysitter and arrange for a surprise picnic?" or "Why don't *we* ever go on long walks through fields of flowers?"

Why? Well...um...because he's a *guy*. Let's face it—with the exception of a few men who thrive on deeply romantic overtures, most men are more concerned with the basics in life: working hard, getting the oil changed, and cleaning out the garage.

But what I've learned in forty-four years of living is there's nothing sexier than a guy who makes sure the oil is changed in the family car before a vacation. There is nothing more attractive than a man who steadfastly goes to work each day to earn a living, or pays the medical insurance on time every month. These things may seem mundane, but they mean everything. It's your husband's version of saying, "I love you madly, my precious darling!"

Foreplay Begins in Your Heart

Women have told men for years that "Foreplay begins in the morning." We've communicated to our guys that it really does matter how they treat us during the day, if they want fulfilling and exciting sex in the evening. But the same advice holds true for women. Our attitudes, the words of our mouths, and our internal dialogue will determine the level of happiness we experience with our husbands. If we mentally or verbally replay our husband's mistakes, insensitive remarks, or financial blunders—we are setting ourselves up for disappointment. We are poisoning our own marriages.

Reclaiming What's Been Lost

Because foreplay really does begin in the heart, especially when it comes to women, we must make a concerted effort to keep our hearts soft and forgiving toward our husbands. I think that most of us would agree that as women, unless our hearts and emotions are engaged, it's a challenge for us to fully open ourselves to our husbands sexually. There are several ways in which we can rekindle the flame of desire and reclaim a soft heart toward our husbands.

1. Overlook his faults.

It's true that marriage can be challenging at times—but it also can be wonderful, fulfilling, comforting, and joyous. If we want to enjoy our marriages, it's important to keep our sense of humor intact and our minds focused on our husband's good qualities. Like the old saying goes, "To have long friendships, you must have a short memory." And one way to have a short memory is by choosing to "overlook" your husband's short-comings.

Why Won't This Man Stop Talking?!

I love the winter Olympics. The snowboarding, the ice-skating, the bobsleds, the cross-country skiing...I enjoy them all. The extreme training, tenacity, and commitment required to qualify for the Olympics captures my imagination and engages my mind and emotions. The favorite part, for me, is the delicious suspense of finding out *who* will win.

My husband, on the other hand, doesn't appreciate the suspenseful aspect of the Olympics at all. During the seventeen-day duration of winter Olympic competition, he'll go online to see the daily results before the games air during primetime.

Every single day of the Olympics he will come home from work and ask me if I want to know who won that day. He knows I don't want to know...I've told him I don't want to know...I've made it clear that under no circumstances do I want to know ahead of time who wins what. But does that stop him from asking? No!

Later on in the evening, as we sit to watch the different competitions, he'll say things like, "I know who wins this." He'll hint at who does well, and who does not. He'll let it slip that a certain athlete won't be doing well in the "Super G" later on in the evening. Ugh! It completely ruins it for me. I had done my best to avoid TV and radio all day, I've closed my eyes when my home page loads on my computer (hoping to avoid the current Olympic standings and scores)—only to have "Bigmouth" come home and *hint* about who wins!

Annoying habits, I've found, are best endured with humor. Obviously, Jeff is out of control when it comes to keeping the Olympic scores to himself. I can approach this in two different ways. I can get angry and take myself *way* too seriously. Or I can laugh at his inane, ridiculous habit of telling me what I've practically begged him not to.

Overlooking another's faults means to literally "look over the top" of the faults to see the person you love standing on the other side. You love your husband. You don't love his faults— but you do love *him*. Remind yourself of all his wonderful qualities. Take his annoying behavior with a "side of humor" and get over yourself. An open, frisky "foreplay" attitude of the heart will be much easier to foster if you're not inwardly seething over your husband's latest annoying foibles.

2. Stop that constant "dripping."

Have you ever known a really critical person? What is your immediate emotional reaction when you think of that person? Negative…right? A critical person just naturally focuses on all that is not up to par. Their expert eye is trained to look for the inferior, defective, and inadequate. They feel compelled to point out the imperfections and substandard behavior of those around them.

But condemnation and criticism do not bring about the desired effect—perfection. The critical person is usually hoping to change the people around them—to transform others into flawless versions of *themselves*. However, the opposite will usually happen. Critical words chip away at a person's confidence, until the inward man finally stands defeated—shoulders slumped and arms hanging limp.

The Word of God has something insightful and humorous to say about a critical or argumentative wife:

A quarrelsome wife is like a constant dripping on a rainy day; restraining her is like restraining the wind or grasping oil with the hand. (Proverbs 27:15–16)

Better to live on a corner of the roof than share a house with a quarrelsome wife. (Proverbs 25:24)

Just think about what this Scripture is saying! According to the Bible, a man would rather live on a corner of his roof—shivering, hungry, and lonely—than be married to a nagging, contentious wife. The Bible compares a wife's arguing and complaining to the constant sound of a downpour on a violently rainy day: grating, incessant, annoying, provoking, and exceedingly irritating.

Criticism may not literally chase a husband up to the roof. But if you regularly pick, nag, argue, and badger, you'll chase him up there emotionally.

If you have a habit of constantly complaining about your husband (either behind his back or to his face), you are demeaning him in your *own* eyes. You are disrespecting him.

Obviously, I'm not talking about open and honest communication (which is a cornerstone of a healthy marriage). I'm referring to a pattern of nagging and criticizing. We must protect how *we* feel about our husbands, so that we can remain available sexually to them. Respect and admiration can quickly be torn down by the words of our mouth. We can choose what we say...we can choose what we think about.

Choose to think respectful thoughts about your husband. Choose to say respectful things to him, and about him. Choose to think about how sexy he is, how much you enjoy making love with him. Recall the times when he has rocked your world. Don't dwell on the negative—dwell on the good, the positive.

Give Him the Key

What's holding you back from giving the garden gate key to the man you love?

According to God's Word, your sex life belongs to both of you. The Lord never intended for *you* to hold all the cards. His perfect plan was for your lovemaking to be shared territory. It might provide hilarious fodder for the plot of a TV sitcom, such as when Ray's wife Debra denies him sex repeatedly on *Everybody Loves Raymond*—complete with every comical excuse under the sun. But truth be told, that kind of behavior is deeply wounding and hurtful to our husbands.

According to survey results in Shaunti Feldhahn's book *For Women Only*, one of men's biggest fears is rejection in the bedroom. Shaunti says:

When we throw out the classic "Not tonight, dear," he hears, "You're so undesirable that you can't compete with a pillow...and I really don't care about what matters deeply to you."

Although we might just be saying we don't want sex *at that point in time*, he hears the much more painful message that we don't want *him*.

Here's what the men themselves said on the survey:

> "She doesn't understand that I feel loved by sexual caressing, and if she doesn't want to, I feel incredible rejection."

> "When she says no, I feel that I am REJECTED. 'No' is not no to sex—as she might feel. It is no to me as I am. And I am vulnerable as I ask or initiate. It's plain and simple rejection."

> "She doesn't understand how even her occasional dismissals make me feel less desirable. I can't resist her. I wish that I, too, were irresistible. She says I am. But her ability to say no so easily makes it hard to believe."

This feeling of personal rejection, and a sense that his wife doesn't really desire him, tends to lead a man into darker waters.[3]

Ladies, being available, ready, and willing is such a simple and easy gift to give our husbands—but to them it's one of the greatest gifts in the world...the key to the garden gate.

Recommended Resources

- Leslie Vernick, *How to Act Right When Your Spouse Acts Wrong* (WaterBrook Press).

- Dr. Ed Wheat and Gloria Okes Perkins, *Love Life for Every Married Couple: How to Fall in Love, Stay in Love, Rekindle Your Love* (Zondervan Publishers).

- Willard F. Harley Jr., *His Needs, Her Needs: Building an Affair-Proof Marriage* (Revell Publishing).

- Gary L. Thomas, *Sacred Influence: What a Man Needs from His Wife to Be the Husband She Wants* (Zondervan Publishers).

- Willard F. Harley Jr., *Love Busters: Overcoming Habits That Destroy Romantic Love* (Revell Press).

- Al Miles, *Violence in Families: What Every Christian Needs to Know* (Augsburg Fortress Publishers).

6

Ta-Da! Look Who You Married

THERE WAS A TIME in my life when I felt as if God super-naturally pulled back a curtain and shouted "Ta-da! Look who you married!" Like the old game show *Let's Make a Deal*, I realized that I had won the most excellent "prize" behind curtain number one. I saw an honorable man, an intelligent man, a caring and steady man. It was at that point in my life that I began to actively revel in the man that was *mine alone*!

Now here's your chance to wake up and take notice of the unique and extraordinary gift that is right in front of your eyes (if you haven't already). Maybe as you sit reading this book, your "gift" is drooling and dreaming in his La-Z-Boy chair. Or perhaps he's just come in the door from golf, smelly and smiling with stories to tell of "birdies" and "par." Or it could be that your "gift" is holed up in his office right now, putting in another long day at work for you and the kids.

It doesn't matter what his career is, how handsome he is, how much hair he has or does *not* have, his hygiene habits, or the circumference of his belly. He's yours—and you *must* revel in that fact, or you are missing a huge blessing in your life!

You may be tempted to make an exception for *your* husband because of his particular idiosyncrasies and faults. However,

I encourage you not to embrace that attitude. Instead, adopt an attitude of faith; ready yourself to receive the blessing that God has for you in chapter 6. Because it's His desire to throw open the curtain of your dulled emotions and muted perceptions, and show you with stunning clarity that the man you always wanted is the one you already have.

So, what are some of the things that can hinder us women from fully enjoying, relishing, and deeply admiring our men? Well, I believe there are four main traps we can easily fall into. Things that can cause us to blindly walk through each day, unaware of the treasure that can be found next to us in bed each night, across the table from us at dinnertime, and beside us in the church pew on Sunday morning. These four traps have the potential to siphon the joy and delight right out of our marriages.

Trap #1: Materialism

Stan and Marie live in a modest three-bedroom, two-bath suburban home with their two boys. They have a postage-stamp-sized front yard with bicycles piled in the driveway, and there are plenty of neighborhood kids for their boys to play with. Stan earns a moderate income as a tax accountant, and Marie stays home with the kids. With a minimal amount of effort, they manage to make their small mortgage payment each month, and even put a little aside for the kids' college fund. They've lived in their cozy neighborhood for the past seven years—busily raising children, enjoying cul-de-sac block parties, and making lifelong friendships.

All was well until...Marie's next-door neighbor Rose excitedly dropped by to share her good news. Rose's husband,

Ethan, recently received a very large pay raise, and they are in the process of selling their home and purchasing a much larger one across town.

It's good timing, too! Rose and Ethan have three small children, with one more on the way—and their brood is bursting at the seams. Rose invites Marie to come with her and check out their brand-new four-bedroom, three-car-garage house, located in the luxurious Montecito Tract.

While Rose is picking out *new* tile, *new* carpet, *new* granite countertops, and *new* appliances for her *new* residence, Marie is quietly fighting the "green monster" within—but smiling on the outside. And as she gazes at the cathedral ceilings in the beautiful model home, she imagines how nice it would be to live in such a spacious house. She would be much happier...her marriage would be much stronger...her kids would be much smarter...and yes—even the dog would be much healthier. Everything would be better! She would exercise more, because after all, who wouldn't want to take long jogs in such beautiful surroundings? And for sure her kids would do better in school—because they would each finally have their own room. And what about all the great meals she could cook with those stainless steel appliances? She would definitely be a much better cook in *that* kitchen!

The seed was thus planted, and Marie faithfully watered it with her prolific imagination, mentally decorating her new home over and over again. She finally decided that she just had to convince her husband, Stan, that their house wasn't nearly big enough. After all, it would be awfully nice to have an exercise room *and* a guest room. Plus, they could sure use the expanded garage space for all their stuff. Yes...the more Marie thought about it, the more she realized that her little family absolutely *needed* that newer, larger home.

As she made her case to Stan later that afternoon, Marie

had a knot in her stomach and tears in her eyes. She explained just how crowded they all were: "You know, Stan, I just don't know how much longer we can all live in these cramped quarters.... The boys need more room to spread out.... You should have *seen* Rose's new backyard!"

Saturday dawned bright and clear, and the whole family jumped in the car to travel across town to take a look around. Of course, Stan loved the three-thousand-square-foot house, and the kids excitedly ran from room to room imagining all the fun they could have in such an expansive home. When Marie walked through the double doors leading to the master bathroom, she practically heard angels singing the hallelujah chorus. She imagined the relaxing baths she could take in the oversize Jacuzzi tub...scented candles surrounding her...classical music playing on the built-in surround-sound stereo...luxurious bubbles caressing her body...the water jets administering a perfect massage...

Later that afternoon, Marie and Stan did their best to "pencil out" their plan to buy a Montecito home. And when the figures just wouldn't add up, Marie proclaimed, "You know Stan, sometimes you just have to trust God and take a leap of faith."

Stan had his doubts, but trusted Marie to "hear from God." Before they knew it, they were moving into their dream home in the Montecito tract. Stan did some tossing and turning over their $3200 mortgage payment, but finally put his nagging doubts aside. He knew they should trust God—after all, "where He guides, He provides."

Each month thereafter was a financial struggle for the family. Stan worked overtime to make up for their added expenses, but it still wasn't enough. Because their children were still small, Stan and Marie agreed that she would continue to be a stay-at-home mom. So...they cut back where they could, but there was never enough to make the mortgage payment each month. Credit card debt ensued...a refinance followed...and finally, they landed on an equity line loan. Now they were actually *spending* what little equity they had accrued in their home. "Shangri-La" quickly turned into "Shouldn't have done it."

The stress between Marie and Stan was palatable, and they both regretted their decision to "buy on faith." The joy that Marie expected to receive from her gorgeous new home was soured by the added anxiety that she and Stan felt. Many of their normal expenses were now being put on the credit cards, and she wondered how they would ever dig out of the financial hole they were in.

If you're living Stan and Marie's life right now, you are in good company. Everyone is susceptible to the charms of materialism. Even the most sensible, cautious people can find themselves caught up in the rush and thrill of buying. Many Americans are overextended financially, living above their means, and living with the day-to-day stress of trying to acquire what they can't afford.

Materialism is a trap that has the potential to steal the simple joys from your marriage. As Christians, we need to actively resist the magnetic pull to buy, buy, buy. Consumers are constantly egged on to upgrade their home, TV, stereo, computer, car, wardrobe, cell phone, iPod, etc. It's upgrade or be left behind, baby: "*What*...you still have dial-up? Wow...I didn't know *anyone* still had dial-up!"

The motto of the world today is "Buy, buy, buy"—but it might better be translated "Fill, fill, fill." Empty people seeking to be "filled" up with something...anything.

But as Christians, we can sincerely and deeply enjoy the gifts that God has given us—without the constant desire for more. In fact, as Christians we can be sure that the bigger, better, brighter, louder, more expensive "things" *won't* fill us up. It's only as we behold and embrace the good gifts that the Lord has given us that we are profoundly "filled." One of the most important gifts a woman can receive from God is her husband. But how do you enjoy the simple, yet profound, blessing of your marriage relationship with a debt guillotine hanging over your head?

The book of Luke has something significant to say about the pursuit of material possessions:

> Then [Jesus] said to them, "Watch out! Be on your guard against all kinds of greed; a man's life does not consist in the abundance of his possessions." (Luke 12:15)

It's important that a husband and wife work together to make a comfortable and happy home for themselves and their children, providing the best they can "afford." But a great wedge will develop in a marriage that constantly suffers the stress of debt. Not only that, but the very *need* that we think can be satisfied only by acquiring the latest, greatest thing will actually be deeply satisfied by the camaraderie and romantic friendship of our husbands.

Let's turn our backs on the lure of materialism and get back to the uncomplicated and simple joys of life. Take a leisurely walk with your husband, holding hands and making small talk. Jump in the car and go for an impromptu drive, finding the best place for a clear view of the sunset. Get back to the simple pleasure of making some popcorn and watching a favorite TV show or movie together.

When was the last time the two of you played a card game together, or dusted off Monopoly for the whole family to enjoy?

Plan a simple picnic of sandwiches, sodas, and chips and take it to the local park. In this fast-paced world, we underestimate the importance of making time for small pleasures. But taking time for simple, enjoyable recreation with our spouse builds intimate companionship.

"Being in the moment" means not taking anything for granted, and enjoying just what your life is today. Ask the Lord to help you enjoy your husband...to enjoy your family...to enjoy the many gifts that He has given you.

You will find it so much easier to enjoy the man God gave you when there isn't the added stress of unpaid bills hanging over your heads. Materialism (and the resulting debt that usually follows) is a trap that will most assuredly steal the "ta-da!" factor from your marriage and siphon the blessing that the Lord intended when you said "I do."

Resist the pull of the world to upgrade. Make it a priority to live within your budget. If you're in over your heads financially, downsize (it's a lot like losing weight—it will take longer to get it off than it took to put it on). Then the rest is easy. With an uncluttered mind and checkbook, you are free to enjoy your man profusely.

Trap #2: Busyness

Jodie is usually awake well before dawn. She can be found most mornings putting in a three-mile workout before the family stirs. After her thirty-minute jog, a quick look at her watch (her ever present taskmaster) indicates that she better get upstairs quickly to wake up her sleepy kids, hop in the shower, and get dressed for work. Then she'll make breakfast...pack lunches...feed the animals...get the kids out the door (don't you dare miss that bus again!)...kiss her husband, Mark, good-bye...quickly zip through Starbucks, and arrive at work just in time for the big sales meeting. Whew! She's out of breath and anxious—and the day has hardly begun!

Her day continues like so many others in a long line of overscheduled days: work, lunch with friends, the afternoon ladies' Bible study, grocery shopping, driving the kids to soccer practice, ballet practice, and a birthday party. Bring the groceries home and put them away...more cooking...more dishes...off to her book club meeting. Home from book club...get the kids to bed (why is it these kids *never* get to bed on time?)...start some laundry (the piles never recede!)...check e-mail...check voice mail...check text messages. Set the alarm clock...set the coffeemaker timer...get out clothes for tomorrow. One last load of laundry in the washer...put the cat out...BED! Ahhhhh, bed! The comfy haven of rest and relaxation. Curling up under her squishy down comforter in her soft flannel jammies, she's ready to fall into blissful slumber.

That is, until Mark reaches for her. "Oh Mark, you can't be serious! You don't know the day I've had."

Sure, he knows the day Jodie had. It's the same day she always has—overly busy and overscheduled.

An overstressed life will undoubtedly siphon the enjoyment right out of our marriages. When we get too busy, our priorities become obscured and the things that are not really very important start taking precedence over the things that are truly important.

So, what's truly important? Our husbands. They should be a priority in our lives—and not just in "theory," like when Jodie brags to her girlfriends at book club, "Mark is *such* a great husband, *so* wonderful...*so* successful...*so* good with the kids. I am *so* lucky to have him!" Rather, Mark should be a true priority in Jodie's life, as in actually *showing* him how she feels about him and loving him in a tangible way (under the covers, later that night). It would help if Jodie remembered that making love to Mark is not her "responsibility," but really, in many ways her blessing and privilege.

Busyness is a trap that is extremely common in our culture. We are always on the run...always on the phone...always on the laptop...always on the PDA...you get the idea. "Self importance" has gripped our society, and we've bought into the idea that we're indispensable, that our friends and business associates can't possibly survive if we're out of cell phone range.

Busyness and overscheduling have become badges of honor that signify a person's importance in this world. But in actuality, we are not indispensable to anyone except our own families. Our husbands and children need the comfort and nurturing that only a wife and mother can bring to a home and family.

We are uniquely necessary to our family's growth and well-being. There may be times when you feel stressed out, unappreciated, and as though you're running around like a chicken with its head cut off. My encouragement to you is to slow down, remove those things in your schedule that are not *absolutely* necessary, and prioritize your life so that there is time to be your husband's friend, lover, parenting partner, and encourager.

Trap #3: Putting Your Children Before Your Husband

When my husband and I were married over twenty years ago, we agreed that we would have only one child. Jeff has two grown daughters from a previous marriage, and he didn't want to continue having kids into his late forties or early fifties. So at the ripe old age of forty-five, he became a dad for the third (and what he thought was the last) time.

I loved being a mom. After having Andrew, I felt like I had found my calling. I mean, obviously motherhood isn't without its challenges, but I genuinely loved and enjoyed being a mom. So of course I wanted one more child. Eventually, my selfless and patient husband agreed to let me have one more. When Andrew was seven and a half years old, Amy was born. What fun I had! I thoroughly immersed myself in her care.

I decided to nurse Amy exclusively, meaning I didn't give her a bottle at all. I completely enjoyed nursing, and continued to do so until Amy was two and a half. Yes, you read that right…two and a half (and no, I don't mean months). I was one of *those* moms that other moms talk about behind their backs: "Can you *believe* she's still nursing that baby? Give me a break! Soon the 'baby' will be walking over, pulling up Paula's shirt, and saying 'Mother, can I please nurse now?'" And actually that wasn't far from the truth. My mom and two older sisters finally said something like, "Enough already—stop nursing that baby!" It was time to wean Amy.

Nursing a little one is a close, intimate activity that requires a lot from you physically as well as emotionally. It's very rewarding—but also taxing. And because of this close contact throughout the day, especially when Amy was very little, the last thing I wanted was *more* physical contact at night. I just didn't want to be touched anymore.

Of course, most husbands understand that caring for a new baby is all consuming, and that they may "temporarily" have to take a lower place on a wife's priority list. But we women need to make sure that our husbands eventually end up back on the top of the priority list. Here's why: Your husband is your life partner. You are *one* with him, and you complete each other.

He is your closest ally, your protector, and your friend. Where you are weak, he is generally strong—and vice versa.

Children are a blessing from God to you and your husband. He gave them to you so that you could raise them in a godly home, love and nurture them, give them wings, and watch them fly! It will be you and your husband who will share all the memories of their growing up years. It will be you and your spouse who will pray for them each night as they make their way in the world. The point being, after the kids fly the coop, who's left? You and your husband, that's who. The man you married all those years ago. He'll be the one standing by your side as the last little chick drives off to college, walks down the aisle, or travels to a foreign country on a mission trip.

Women can easily become obsessed with their children's activities, appetites, material needs, wants, desires, and friends. Sometimes a woman will rearrange her dinner menu because little Johnny has decided he doesn't like chicken—but will resist making her husband's favorite meatloaf because "It's just too much trouble." She may be willing to rearrange her entire weekend schedule so Johnny can attend Nathan's birthday party—but resist rearranging her schedule to accommodate her husband's fishing trip with his buddies.

Women can be guilty of "preferring" their children's desires and needs over their husband's. My mother was raised in the 1940s and refers to the children of today as "adored and glorified."

As Christian women, I genuinely believe that you and I are earnestly attempting to *not* spoil our kids—which is hard to do in the "me, me, me" society in which we live. But we are making the effort to go against the flow: teaching our children from the Bible, taking them to church, and in some cases, cutting back on luxuries in order to afford Christian school. And one of the best safeguards against overindulging our kids is by making our husband "king" of the home instead of little Johnny.

Trap #4: Selfishness

Polly, a beautiful yet untalented wannabe singer, dejectedly walked off the stage with the scathing words of *American Idol*'s Simon Cowell still ringing in her ears: "You were simply terrible. You have no talent whatsoever!" Later, while mascara runs down Polly's cheeks, a camera catches her reaction to news that she has "no talent whatsoever." She looks straight into the lens and with heartfelt passion repeats the words that numerous other contestants have comforted themselves with all afternoon: "That's okay, because everything happens for a reason."

Yeah, Polly. The reason is that *you can't sing*! There really is no cosmic, universal design to bring you the fame you believe destiny has planned for you. *American Idol* rejected you because you aren't good at singing. That's all.

The ridiculous saying "Everything happens for a reason" is quoted by celebrity and simpleton alike, and conveniently takes personal responsibility out of the equation. For example, if Uncle Joe ate and drank nothing but nachos, pizza, hot dogs, and bourbon, and then ended up with clogged arteries and a heart attack, by Polly's logic we would have to say, "Oh, you poor thing! Just remember, Uncle Joe—everything happens for a reason."

In reality, there really is no mysterious cosmic reason Joe has clogged arteries. Uncle Joe's heart stopped working correctly because he didn't eat life-giving foods. It's just plain old "sowing and reaping" being played out. That doesn't negate the fact that a merciful God will stay close to us during our reaping, because He will. He loves us, even when we've stupidly sown weeds in our lives. If we have repentant and teachable hearts, He will comfort, heal, and rescue us time and again.

Reaping and Sowing

Stephanie lost interest in her husband, Kevin, several years ago, but trudged on for the sake of the children.

For one thing, Kevin put on some weight over the last few years and now sported quite the beer belly. For another, he spent an inordinate amount of time at work each week, and then went golfing every Saturday with his friends. In addition to all that, Kevin spent every evening flipping channels or sleeping soundly on the couch, completely oblivious to Stephanie's growing resentment.

It had been months since they made love, and even longer since they discussed the state of their marriage. Oh, sure— Kevin still took care of his responsibilities, working hard each week and bringing home a paycheck, spending time with the kids, and taking care of the cars and the yard. But how long had it been since he brought her flowers or candy, or took her out to a nice restaurant? How long since he skipped golf to spend a Saturday with her? Her *needs* were not being met by Kevin, and he didn't even seem to be trying to make her happy anymore.

Because of her many disappointments in Kevin and his inability to make even some of the small changes she requested, Stephanie felt justified in deflecting his repeated advances for intimacy. And who could blame her? After all, should she really be expected to get physical with a man whom she now found repugnant?

They were at a stalemate: Stephanie accusing and criticizing, Kevin retreating and hibernating.

Then one day Stephanie arrived home from a weekend visit (and bashing session) with her mother to find Kevin gone.

Later that week, while out to lunch with friends, a disconsolate Stephanie picked at her food while her girlfriends told her, "Stephanie, you're better off without Kevin! Remember, *everything happens for a reason.*"

But their words sounded shallow and meaningless to Stephanie's ears. Stephanie missed Kevin terribly. She remembered how intelligent Kevin was, how witty and clever, how responsible and trustworthy, how good with their children.

She realized that she still loved Kevin.

Her eyes newly opened, Stephanie sought reconciliation with Kevin, and they began the process of working through their problems. Now they talk, apologize, understand, forgive, pray, and make love.

Selfishness blinded Stephanie to the greatness of the man that was hers alone, and dictated that she seek her own happiness.

Selfishness will demand that *your* needs be met first. Selfishness cannot be bothered to sow seeds of love, trust, and kindness. Instead it demands, "Meet *my* needs first; *then* I'll sow seeds of love." Selfishness wants a shortcut to the reward of kind and giving behavior. When we are needs focused, we circumvent God's avenue of blessing in our lives.

> Do not be deceived: God cannot be mocked. A man reaps what he sows. The one who sows to please his

sinful nature, from that nature will reap destruction; the one who sows to please the Spirit, from the Spirit will reap eternal life. Let us not become weary in doing good, for at the proper time we will reap a harvest if we do not give up. (Galatians 6:7–9)

What are you sowing into your marriage? The Bible plainly tells us that God won't be mocked, and that a man reaps what he sows—and yet many times we act as if the Lord doesn't really mean it.

Perhaps you are tempted to assume that the Lord will make an exception to this spiritual law because you're married to an especially difficult man. But the law of sowing and reaping stands true in all situations, and it will be God's wonderful grace that will enable us to fulfill that law.

Consistently bad life choices will lead to a consistently bad life. That one statement could change your whole future! A person that is constantly in a "storm" and literally bounces from one disaster to another is sometimes guilty of making consistently bad life choices—sowing seeds of destruction and reaping turmoil. For example:

If you spend money you do not have, you will be in debt (sow greed—reap sleeplessness).

If you eat copious amounts of junk food, you will get fat and unhealthy (sow gluttony—reap obesity).

If you drive too fast, you will eventually crash your car (sow impatience—reap injury or death).

If you repeatedly call in sick for work, you will eventually get fired (sow laziness—reap shame).

If you disregard your husband's feelings and focus only on getting your own needs met, you may become a divorce statistic (sow neglect—reap disunity).

I can just hear some of you right now saying, "But Paula, I *do* have needs! I want to be noticed by my husband, to be loved, to be heard. I need him to pay attention to the things that matter to me...to help more with the kids...to stay home more...to go to church with us...to be the head of the family... to do things around the house...to pray with the kids...to work harder...be more attentive, etc."

I'm not suggesting that you stop communicating with your husband and ignore the problems between you. But I am saying it's possible that you have become a need machine, and that at this point in your marriage your husband has pushed the mute button. He can see your mouth moving, but the sound is turned off. Why? Because he *knows* you have needs—that much is clear to him. But sometimes the way in which we women communicate our needs to our husbands can make them feel like a failure. So...I am proposing that we go about this in an entirely different way—the biblical way!

I propose that we do our best to sow love, faithfulness, kindness, romance, attentiveness, and joyfulness into our marriages, regardless of what we feel we deserve. Galatians 6:9 tells us not to become weary in doing good, because we will reap a harvest if we don't give up. God's Word is true. It's always true—100 percent of the time. That means, in one way or another, we absolutely will reap a harvest if we sow good seeds in our marriages.

I believe that you will reap a harvest in your marriage if you make the decision to sow loving words and actions into it. Even in the exceptional cases where this does not happen, you will still reap directly from the Lord with an increase of His presence in your life, and the joy and blessing of giving.

What to Sow, What to Sow?

Most of you are somewhat familiar with the basics of gardening. You know, then, that whatever *kind* of seed you put in the ground is the *kind* of plant that will grow. If you plant carrot seeds in your vegetable garden, by summer you'll be pulling delicious, crunchy carrots out of the ground. If you sow tomato seeds when the weather turns warm, by the dog days of summer you'll be reaping bright red, homegrown tomatoes. If you're crazy enough to sow dandelions in your flower garden, you will soon reap dandelions. If you're foolish enough to sow crabgrass in your immaculate front yard, the crabgrass will soon choke out the "good" grass and overrun the entire lawn. It really does matter what you sow.

Crabby Women Sow Crabgrass

Olivia's at it again, and everyone knows to stay out of her way.

Her daughter, Cindy, is holed up in her room, trying to escape to her happy place by listening to the radio and reading *Narnia;* her husband, Brian, has retreated to the garage with his cell phone and is making covert plans to go out bowling with the guys. Olivia's neighbor Jackie was seen practically running from the house after coming over to borrow some Coffee-mate. Olivia's son, Jeffrey, just peeled out of driveway in his Saturn, desperate to be anywhere but there. And Olivia's sister Jill cancelled their lunch date for later that day, after only a forty-five-second-long conversation with her.

What's wrong with poor Olivia, you ask? Is she wildly contagious with a deadly disease—bleeding from the eyes and coughing up great gobs of phlegm? Maybe she's gone crazy and is chasing people around the neighborhood with a semi-automatic rifle? No, no...it's nothing like that. It's worse, actually. Olivia has PMS.

Some women dominate their entire household with their out-of-control mood swings. A dark cloud descends upon the family home several days before her period, raining down wrath, criticism, sarcasm, and depression. She claims to be as much a victim as the rest of the family by her PMS. She maintains that *her* PMS is worse than the average woman's and that honestly, she has no ability to control it! The family is forced to tiptoe around her, doing their best to avoid any kind of disagreement with the PMS Czar.

My mother has some wisdom when it comes to PMS and mood swings. When my two sisters and I were at the teenage stage in life, my mom didn't put up with a whole lot of nonsense. If we tried to use the excuse of being in a "bad mood" because of our period, she would say, "Oh snap out of it! There's no such thing as a 'bad mood.' What's that? What exactly is a 'bad mood'? How ridiculous! You're just choosing to act ugly, and trying to get away with it. If a guy you liked stopped by the house right now you would put a big smile on your face, and try to impress him with your most sparkling conversation."

To prove my mom's point—how many of you pulled the PMS card when you were still *dating* your husband? Yeah... that's right...none of you did. Is it because nobody ever has PMS before they are married? I think not. I believe it's because we were choosing to control our mood swings when we were still trying to catch our husbands. It was only when the fish was safely gutted and tucked in the freezer that we pulled PMS out of the tackle box.

It's selfish to dominate and control the entire household with PMS, or any kind of mood swing. As Christian women I believe we should expect more out of ourselves than that (and yes, I'm preaching to myself here, too). We get to *choose* the kinds of seeds that we are sowing into our husband's life. It is not okay to claim we have no control over our PMS mood swings.

I'll say it again: We get to *choose* how we act. Sometimes we just have to make the choice to act kind and loving regardless of how we feel. In other words, it's okay to act pleasant and joyful even when we don't feel that way. In fact, I contend that if you act pleasant and joyful long enough, you will eventually begin to *feel* that way.

When you are deciding what to plant in your garden each summer, you carefully choose those vegetables that your family enjoys eating. If everyone hates zucchini squash, obviously you aren't going to plant it. But if you all enjoy fresh homegrown tomatoes, then that's what you'll grow.

In the same way, our husbands are worthy of our respectful and kind treatment all month long, and they will thrive like sunny, well-watered gardens if tended correctly.

It's funny...with just a little tender loving care, men generally rise to the occasion, doing their very best to meet our needs. If we take our attention off what *he's not doing right*, and put our attention back where it belongs—on our own behavior—then we will find that the rest takes care of itself.

- If you consistently treat your husband kindly (despite fluctuating hormones), your husband will be grateful and will richly appreciate you (sow self*less*ness—reap appreciation).
- If you regularly make yourself available sexually to your husband, he will be satisfied and happy, and more than ready to meet your needs (sow romance—reap *your* needs being met).

- If you provide your husband with a nice hot dinner after work each day, or take the time to pack him a lunch for work, he'll be well fed and happy, feeling important to you (sow food preparation—reap a loving husband).
- If you hold your tongue and resist the urge to nag or criticize, he will reclaim his manhood and become "the man you always wanted" (sow restraint—reap husband-esteem).
- If you initiate sex with your husband from time to time, he will feel like he's your "prize" and respond with pure joy (sow friskiness—reap marital delight).
- If you sow verbal appreciation of all he does for you and the kids, he will never feel taken for granted again, and you will have new eyes for all his hard work (sow praise—reap gratitude).

God wants to give you a "gift" today. He wants to pull back the curtain of your needs and *emotions* (both will lie to you), revealing to you the unique greatness of the man you married. The specifications of your particular husband do not matter—fat, thin, talkative, quiet, sick, healthy, old, young, smart, not so smart, rich, poor...none of that matters.

What does matter is that you sit up and take notice of your husband today. Prepare yourself to be "wowed" as God reveals this man to you in a new way. *Now* is the time to brace yourself for the curtain pull. It's gonna be good...you should probably be sitting down for this...get ready now...are you ready? Okay...here it comes:

Ta-da! Look who you married!

7

The Freedom of Forgiveness

FORGIVENESS IS A JOURNEY requiring tenacity and obedience. It's a pilgrimage that will lead the traveler from the jagged peaks of offense, through the scorching desert of distress, until he arrives safely at the resplendent reservoir of peace and release.

This journey is not for the faint of heart or the easily discouraged. It's for the lionhearted pilgrim who is willing to obey God's Word at all costs, laying down the desire for recompense. Let's follow a fair maiden named Annabel on her journey, and I'll show you what I mean.

There once was a lovely young woman named Annabel who had come to live in a sinister and forsaken place called The Land of Records. Wicked King Natas ruled this kingdom with an iron fist of oppression—fear being the principal tool wielded to control and subjugate the inhabitants of the empire. Fear of what, you may ask? Well, fear of leaving...fear of staying...and fear of living in The Land of Records...but mostly, fear of losing the Book.

But I'm getting ahead of myself. Back to Annabel.

Annabel's small home was furnished in muted shades of

gray, and stood at the end of a desolate, treeless street with its back to the sun. Life was bleak in The Land of Records, and each day was almost exactly as the day before. There was only one kind of food allowed in the city—"bitter bread." It was as its name designates: bitter. So bitter, in fact, that it stung Annabel's tongue when she ate it, and she would burn inside for hours afterward. But when you're hungry, you'll eat anything.

Every resident in The Land of Records had one thing in common—they each owned a very valuable, very large book called *The Wounds*. This ponderous record book was leather-bound and gold leafed, with a jewel-encrusted cover. Nobody ever went anywhere without their book, and each person guarded it as if it were their very life.

Some people's books had grown so large that they had to haul them around in a wooden cart. Thankfully, Annabel was still able to carry her book in her arms, although at forty-three pounds it was starting to become quite cumbersome—her back was constantly sore from the strain. But setting the book down even for a moment was unthinkable, as it was her most prized possession. The occupants of The Land of Records were constantly reminded by the nefarious King Natas of its irreplaceable value.

One day Annabel received a letter from her beloved husband, Joshua, who resided in Liberty Kingdom. In the letter, he begged her once again to come home. Joshua wrote that he and their daughter, Genevieve, missed Annabel terribly. He needed his wife back, and Genevieve needed her mother. As Annabel read the letter from Joshua, tears streamed down her face. She remembered the secure feeling of his strong arms around her. She recalled her husband's smell...his laugh...and even his whiskered face when he kissed her good night. She ached for her family.

Oh how she missed her life in Liberty Kingdom. She was born and raised there...met and married Joshua there...delivered her baby girl there. She remembered the rolling green hills, the miles and miles of fertile farmland, the pristine city streets, and the charming shops and restaurants. The sun shone brilliantly in Liberty Kingdom, and the sky usually hosted a handful of cotton candy clouds. She could almost taste the fresh bread, baked daily in the many cafes along the main street. Silken streams meandered throughout the kingdom, and the air was cool, fresh, and clean. Annabel's home—at least the one she used to live in with her husband and daughter—was situated high on a hill overlooking the city. It was simple and beautiful, and she missed it terribly.

What she missed most—even more than her beloved family—was King Rapha. He was the glorious and righteous leader of Liberty Kingdom. Everyone loved him and he loved everyone. As he walked through the streets, children and adults alike would clamor to see him, touch him, worship him, and hug him. He was beautiful beyond words and even the thought of him now thrilled her heart and made her long to worship him once more. King Rapha's touch was known to heal any sickness, and just a few comforting words from his mouth could bring lifelong peace to a troubled mind. After living under the relentless oppression and torment of wicked King Natas, Annabel had almost forgotten the boundless joy and glory of living a life of freedom in Liberty Kingdom.

Joshua's letter propelled Annabel into a state of indecision and confusion as she contemplated her future. To leave The Land of Records seemed unthinkable—the price was simply too high. It was common knowledge that under no circumstance was anyone allowed to enter Liberty Kingdom with *The Wounds* in their possession. But how could she leave a thing of such importance and value behind? The very reason that she now lived in The Land of Records had to do with her beloved book.

Several years ago, she was covertly offered the book by a passing King Natas as she stood looking out the lattice gate by the Wall of Redemption that circled Liberty Kingdom. He had offered her the beautiful book just when she needed it most. And after examining the bejeweled cover, leather binding, and gold leaf pages, she decided to take it (just for a little while, mind you). She needed a place to record several terrible and grievous wounds that she had recently suffered at the hands of others. For while it was true that Liberty Kingdom was a wonderful place to live, its inhabitants were only human—and we all know the tragic sins and heartbreaking wounds that human beings can sometimes inflict upon each other.

When it was discovered that Annabel was secretly in possession of *The Wounds*, she was given the option of discarding the book forever or leaving Liberty Kingdom that very day. But by then the book meant too much to Annabel; giving it up, it seemed to her, would mean giving up her very soul.

That was a long time ago, and her book had expanded considerably over the years. More transgressions were remembered by Annabel, and more wounds were dug up and exposed (with the help of King Natas). And with each new entry, Annabel received another jewel on the cover of her book (which greatly enhanced its beauty, but also added to its weight). To leave her book in The Land of Records and go back empty-handed to Liberty Kingdom would seem a waste of the past few years. But as she lay down to rest that night, she couldn't get Joshua, Genevieve, and especially King Rapha out of her mind.

After tossing and turning all night long, Annabel made the decision to go home—book or no book.

In the morning Annabel packed her belongings and began

the long journey back to her homeland. Each day she walked and walked, and each night she slept fitfully on the hard ground, dreaming about her future.

The day finally came when she could see Liberty Kingdom on the horizon. Oh, how her spirits rose! She quickened her pace toward her final destination. Almost there...almost home...almost loved.

In the distance she could see the majestic Wall of Redemption that encircled the city. As she drew nearer, she came upon a tall sentry conscientiously guarding the entrance. She greeted him in a friendly manner and tried to enter as if she had only been out for a lovely stroll through the mountainside. But the gatekeeper could see by her dress, demeanor, and the very large book she carried that she was no day traveler.

"Hello, young woman. I am Sentry Clean Slate. How may I assist you this fine day?"

"Ah...oh...hello, Sentry. I would like to pass through the gate, if you don't mind."

"No, my dear, I certainly don't mind, but you cannot bring *The Wounds* into Liberty Kingdom. We discovered a long time ago that this book will cause an outbreak of anger, bitterness, sickness, and pain among our residents, and we never allow a person to enter the kingdom with it."

"But sir, you don't understand; *my* book of *Wounds* is very, very valuable and necessary. Without it I would be vulnerable. It's important that I remember all the wounds inflicted upon me, so that I can guard myself against future hurts. In addition to that, it is embedded with many fine jewels and is priceless in its worth."

Sentry Clean Slate took the very large book from Annabel's hands and carefully examined the jewels. "No, my friend, these are not precious stones. They are only fool's gold, sea glass, and bits of shiny rock and quartz. This book has no power to protect you from future hurts, but will only cause pain by the remembrance of the past. And have you forgotten that King Rapha will surely heal any wound that your future may hold?

"My dear, you have been deceived into thinking that this book of *Wounds* held safety and value—but it has only robbed you of your joy and peace…your husband's love…your child's embrace…and even your King's benevolent compassion. This book has locked you away from all you truly value, has fed you the bread of bitterness, and has stolen your future from you. To pass through the gate into Liberty Kingdom, you must relinquish the right to own this book and throw it into the River of Forgetfulness."

Annabel had been robbed for long enough. She could see the city's golden beauty through the lattice of the gate and could almost hear her husband's voice calling for her. In her mind's eye, she could imagine Genevieve's delight at having a mommy to hold her again—and what would it be like to once again worship at the feet of her beloved King Rapha?

With one fell swoop, Annabel pulled the large book from the sentry's hand and flung it with all her strength and might into the River of Forgetfulness. Smiling for the first time in years, Annabel bid farewell to Sentry Clean Slate, gathered up her long skirt in her hands, and ran for the gate.

Oh, the marvelous joy and liberation of forgiveness! If you can identify with Annabel—if you, too, have been living in the penitentiary of unforgiveness—trust me that there is nothing better than the sweet freedom and glorious relief of surrendering your book of *Wounds* to King Rapha.

If you've lived in The Land of Records for any time at all, this trade may seem impossible at first. But it's not impossible! This is your moment. This is a new beginning. This is the time to let go of the hurts, the wounds, and the scars. Let Jesus Christ wash away the memories of the things you've suffered. Let Him bring redemption to the difficult things that have happened to you in your life. He loves you, my dear friend. He sees the prison you've been living in, and He has come to rescue you and bring you triumphantly into Liberty Kingdom.

Let me start by laying a biblical foundation for the subject of forgiveness. God's Word is inerrant in its authority and can be trusted to provide accurate answers to all of life's questions.

Why Must I Forgive?

1. Out of obedience to God's Word.

"For if you forgive men when they sin against you, your heavenly Father will also forgive you. But if you do not forgive men their sins, your Father will not forgive your sins." (Matthew 6:14–15)

I think it's very significant that the Lord gave no exceptions to this rule of forgiveness. There's no "wiggle room" in this Scripture. It's cut-and-dried: If you want to be forgiven, you must forgive.

My pastor, Eric Stovesand, recently preached a sermon on peacemaking that shed some light on the subject of forgiveness. He used an analogy of the anti-virus program that's installed on his computer. From time to time this program initiates a computer sweep to check for any new virus threats. And inevitably, after the sweep is completed, it discovers that there are several new threats to his computer. Once the "virus check" program has indicated there are hazardous viruses at-tempting to attack the computer, Pastor Eric has to choose to delete those viruses from his system.

He went on to explain that conflict is like an "idol check" in our hearts: It will be followed by either resolution and for-giveness or irresolution and unforgiveness.

He taught that going through conflict with someone acts as an "idol check" on your heart. If the conflict triggers for-giveness—even in the painful scenario where there can be no resolution—you have the comfort knowing that your system is running idol-free.

But if the conflict triggers bitterness, gossip, and unfor-giveness, then the "idol check" has discovered a new threat to your heart—one that must be handled immediately if you don't want to find yourself living in The Land of Records.

The idol in question could be the need to feel justified, the desire to be treated fairly, the necessity to be the victim, or the longing for a heartfelt apology. Pastor Eric explained that even being too sensitive can be the idol that is unearthed dur-ing the "idol check" of conflict. He explained that being overly sensitive in conflict is similar to coddling your feelings like a precious little kitten—tucked safely into your chest...pro-tected from any outside intrusion...your little baby that you speak tenderly to.

Once the idol check of conflict has exposed a problem, we must take that virus to God, ask Him to remove it, and request that He eliminate any lingering propensity to indulge that particular idol.

The next step is obeying God's scriptural direction con-cerning forgiveness: to forgive the person, ask for forgiveness, or both. When we do that, we invite God's wisdom, peace, and presence into any troubling situation.

2. To achieve a productive prayer life.

"Therefore I tell you, whatever you ask for in prayer, believe that you have received it, and it will be yours. And when you stand praying, if you hold anything against anyone, forgive him, so that your Father in heaven may forgive you your sins." (Mark 11:24–25)

About a year after my inappropriate relationship with the pastor ended, the Lord used a continuous drought of His presence during my prayer time as a catalyst for forgiveness in my life.

One day, after another "leaden heaven" kind of prayer time, I cried out to God in frustration. He revealed to me two very consequential things about prayer: The first was that *I* must forgive those who wound me if I was to expect answers to prayer (noted in the Scripture above). The second was that God wouldn't accept my offering of prayer unless I went to the people *I* wounded and sought their forgiveness (see Matthew 5:23–24).

I knew all along that there were specific people I had wounded deeply during that dreadful time in my life. And while I certainly felt badly about hurting them, I didn't think the Lord was going to make me apologize individually to them.

But after praying about it, I felt strongly encouraged to seek reconciliation with the individuals that my actions had especially hurt. I started by asking forgiveness from the church elders. The Holy Spirit revealed to me the depth of their disappointment and hurt over the damage that my indiscretion had caused their beloved church. They had labored to start that little church, given their time and money and labor for the people of that fellowship. The problem was not that they were mad at me. The problem was that my actions had hurt that little flock.

Next, I wrote letters to several women that I had deeply wounded by my actions. These letters were not easy to write, but were an important step of obedience for me.

After seeking forgiveness from those I had wounded, I then had to make the decision to forgive those who had wounded me during that time. This was more difficult because my extreme guilt had buried the fact that I was hurt by the gossiping of people in my church. I was immersed in an ocean of guilt and rejection—and honestly, I didn't know the depth of my wounds until I allowed the Lord to show me. But the truth was I was devastated by the gossip. It wasn't until I allowed the Holy Spirit to excavate my real feelings that I realized how much unforgiveness I really had. And it was in that place of honesty that I could make a determined decision to forgive.

3. To let go of the desire to avenge.

> "Do not repay anyone evil for evil. Be careful to do what is right in the eyes of everybody. If it is possible, as far as it depends on you, live at peace with everyone. Do not take revenge, my friends, but leave room for God's wrath, for it is written: 'It is mine to avenge; I will repay,' says the Lord." (Romans 12:17–21)

The desire for retribution is a completely normal reaction to being wronged, but as Christians we make the choice to live by a higher law. We are now living by the law of love and we are willingly subject to God's Word.

One of the main reasons people refuse to forgive is their

sense of righteous indignation. Believing (incorrectly) that they are behaving with complete fairness and equity, they collect jewels of "justice" on their book of *Wounds*. "Just letting it go" feels like they're making it way too easy on the sinner—as though the offender will be let off the hook and given carte blanche to sin again.

On the contrary—forgiving someone means that you put them fully in the hands of the living God to let Him punish, vindicate, or pardon as He wills it. By forgiving the offender, you are not putting your faith in your own ability to exact justice, but resting your faith firmly in a righteous and faithful God. Pastor Eric likes to say that "Unforgiveness is the poison you drink hoping the other person will die."

Another reason people resist forgiving their transgressor is for "self-protection." Like Annabel, they wrongly believe that remembering past wounds will somehow shield them from future hurts. Self-preservation drives them to cling to the memories in order to deflect further rejection, shame, scorn, and hurt. But the memories will only hurt them further, as well as keep them from the healing touch of King Rapha (note: *Jehovah Rapha* is an Old Testament name meaning "The Lord, my healer").

My two kids are almost eight years apart in age. When they were younger, I would occasionally ask Andrew to babysit. Usually I would arrive home to my son bitterly complaining about his little sister's naughty behavior. In his adolescent mind he felt completely justified meting out punishment—typically a very wordy tongue lashing, followed by a very long time-out. So you can bet that when he gave me a complete rundown of her unpleasant antics and the ensuing penalty, I *did not* continue her discipline. Why? Because he had already taken matters into his own hands. She had already been punished (thoroughly).

He could have chosen to wait until I got home, told me what offense had been committed, and then let *me* punish her appropriately. But in his anger and frustration he did it himself, causing a rift in their relationship.

Romans 12:17–21 instructs us to step aside and let God dish out the punishment. He doesn't want rifts in our relationships, so He wisely tells us to not repay evil for evil. He wants us to "leave room for His wrath" by forgiving and prayerfully leaving the offender in His hands.

But You Don't Know What I've Been Through!

Many times when I've spoken to a group of women on forgiveness, a woman will say to me privately afterward, "But Paula, you don't know what I've been through!" I usually reply, "Well, you don't know what *I've* been through!"

You see, everyone's been through something. Like many of you, I've had to forgive some tough things in my life, too. What the ladies see before them as I'm speaking on forgiveness is the *by-product* of forgiveness. They see the joyful countenance of a person who has forgiven others and knows the freedom of being forgiven. Those who struggle with unforgiveness feel as though they're watching the wondrous freedom enjoyed by the inhabitants of Liberty Kingdom from outside the city gate—and are uncertain how to enter. They incorrectly assume that those who live free from bitterness haven't forgiven offenses as deeply wounding and grievous as those they're struggling with.

I was at a women's retreat in Southern California recently, where the pastor's wife, Betty, gave the most inspirational testimony on forgiveness that I have ever heard.

Betty told about how her precious one-and-a-half-year-old granddaughter had been murdered by her father (Betty's son-in-law). The man was ultimately sentenced to a lengthy prison term. Due to the tragedy and betrayal she had sustained, Betty's grieving daughter was unable to care for her little boy. Betty and her husband are now raising their grandson, and will do so until he is grown.

What's remarkable is how Betty and her husband have made the courageous decision to minister to their son-in-law while he's in prison. They've not only completely forgiven him, but each week she mails her husband's sermon notes to the prison (audio recordings are not allowed). They regularly allow their grandson to visit with his dad on the phone, and they pray for their son-in-law consistently.

Betty is a delightfully happy woman. She ministers at women's retreats with depth and compassion, and she relays an important message on forgiveness to the women of this generation. If you were to meet her today, you would have no indication of the horrendous, devastating, and life-changing events that she has been through. Betty lives in Liberty Kingdom, and King Rapha has healed her of her wounds.

Unforgiveness—the Great Marriage Divider

There is unfettered and joyous emancipation through the door of forgiveness. Liberty awaits the fearless sojourner who moves forward without keeping a record of past hurts and offenses.

Respect, trust, and enjoyment of the husband God gave you will be almost impossible if you are bound by unforgiveness. Holding on to offenses will quickly destroy and undermine the foundation of your marriage. You may still be living in the same home and sharing the same last name, but it's like living in a home with a cracked foundation—the least little storm could knock it down.

If you're a woman who's in the habit of keeping your husband's "rap sheet" close at hand, carefully tracking his every iniquity, then your heart is caged by fear and self-pity. Here are some of the detrimental effects you will incur.

Fear

Fear manipulates our emotions, causing us to believe that we can control the severity of future hurts by holding on to past wounds. Fear causes us to cling to the memory of past emotional injuries like a shield to deflect future trauma.

But in reality, fear will only back us into an emotional prison cell, and we'll eventually find ourselves living our lives in an apprehensive, negative, and suspicious manner.

As I sat today at my computer writing, I was distracted by some horses at the ranch adjacent to our home. They frolicked and ran around all morning. It was so cute to watch them race back and forth in their expansive pasture, bucking, leaping, and even lying on their backs and wriggling all around. Our neighborhood horses sure enjoy their freedom.

But there are other horses on the ranch that, for whatever reason, are not allowed to roam free. They are kept separate in small corrals that do not afford much space to move about. There is definitely no room to run, play, wriggle on their backs, or "horse around" with their buddies.

While it's a simplistic analogy, it's actually a perfect example of the radical difference between those who know the freedom of forgiveness and those who do not. Because, as I've said before, unforgiveness will cage your heart and rob you of the joy of living, the joy of loving, and the joy of your husband's company.

A free heart is one that loves completely, forgives easily, enjoys abundantly, and appreciates unconditionally. A bound heart is one which loves suspiciously, harbors quickly, resents immediately, and undervalues consistently.

Self-Pity

The fact that self-pity is a "bad" thing seems obvious from the start. Self-pity fuels the fire of deception and keeps it burning bright. It is deception to believe that we have the right *not* to forgive someone who has wounded us. But because of its insidious and deceptive nature, self-pity can easily worm its way into our lives—disguised as a friend—and develop a stronghold in our minds.

Self-pity will arrive camouflaged as a comrade and ally. It will beckon us with the promise of comfort, as a cushy pillow beckons after a hard day's work. "You poor thing," it soothes. "Nobody can possibly understand how profoundly you've been hurt."

Self-pity leads us on a journey that reminds us of all the scars and anguish we've experienced at the hands of others... all the emotional distress we've endured...and on and on.

Self-pity beckons us down the path of narcissism, where we sit as queen over our own lives, and God's help is hard to find. If we don't resist, we'll soon find ourselves believing that we are far more important than we really are, that our hurts are far worse than they really are.

If self-pity is allowed to whisper sweet nothings in our ear long enough, we will become convinced that in *our* case, forgiveness is simply not an option—that the hurt was too deep, the offense too grievous.

My friend Emily had an incident years ago that showed her the true meaning of forgiveness. It started off minor enough, but eventually escalated into a full-blown argument.

She and her husband had borrowed a mattress for their little boy while serving as missionaries in a foreign country. The mattress came with a plastic cover that was uncomfortable for their child to sleep on. So, on the advice of a friend, Emily finally took the mattress cover off because it had been many months since their little boy had wet his bed.

Of course you know what happened next. Her little guy had an accident, and Emily was left wondering how to clean the mattress properly. She decided that the best course of action would be to set it out in the sun. That's when the problems started.

Emily's husband, Paul, saw the mattress sitting out and grilled Emily: *Just how did this happen?* He was appalled by the silliness of her decision to take the mattress cover off—and said so…and said so…and said so (ever had one of those kinds of arguments?).

She was trying to defend her actions when she sensed the Lord asking her to be quiet and stop defending herself (it was getting her nowhere, anyway). On the inside she felt crushed and attacked, but on the outside she remained calm and just let her husband rail.

She told me recently that she learned two valuable lessons that day.

First, she was reminded of the goodness and character of Christ. *He* was completely innocent and didn't defend himself against His accusers—not even once.

Second, the Lord taught her that if she would stop defending herself when falsely accused (or, in this case, when faced with overreaction by her husband), the Lord would be her defender.

I think sometimes we're so busy defending ourselves when we argue with our husbands that we become mired in a war of words and things quickly escalate. Self-pity, combined with the victim mentality, will often goad us into voraciously defending ourselves rather than listening, discussing, and forgiving.

He Didn't Say "I'm Sorry"

I was seething!

I stared stonily out the passenger window as our car flew down the highway. My husband and I had just exchanged some angry words. He obviously did not realize that his young bride was used to getting her own way. As the landscape passed by, I silently vowed not to speak to him until he apologized for his unkind remarks.

The only problem with my plan was how the "silent treatment" was making me feel inside. My newfound Christianity seemed to be interfering with the usual coddling that I liked to give my resentment and anger.

Then the Lord began to deal with me, requiring my forgiveness. And after squirming in my seat for a while, I finally relented. "Okay, Lord, I don't want to...but with your help I will forgive Jeff for disagreeing with me."

And then the shock! Forgiving *him* was not what God asking me to do. He was requiring that I ask Jeff to forgive *me*!

Hello? What did I do wrong?

After stewing for a few more minutes, I began to recognize my own part in the argument. And during that car ride/prayer time, the Lord plainly showed me that I had a real intolerance for being disagreed with by my husband.

So, in what I thought was a beautiful and benevolent

display of humility, I turned to my husband and said, "Honey, I'm sorry"—fully expecting that he would then say he was sorry, too.

He turned to me. "Yeah, okay."

Yeah, okay? *Yeah, okay?* Where was the "Paula, baby, honey, sweetheart, I'm sorry, too! Please forgive me, my kitten"?

I felt set up by the Lord (and in truth, I probably was). He taught me a valuable lesson that day on forgiveness—one that has taken me through almost twenty-two years of marriage. The lesson was this: Don't apologize to *get* an apology.

You don't meet in the middle with an apology; rather, you choose to ask forgiveness for your sin, and at the same time choose to overlook and forgive the other person's sin. Period, end of subject.

Certainly, apologizing goes a long way in making amends and healing offenses—but it's not tit for tat ("I'll say *I'm* sorry if you say *you're* sorry"). Forgiveness is a gift with no strings attached. It's a gift to the offender, a gift to yourself, and a gift to God (one which He requires you to give).

Many years ago, my dear friends Mike and Jan had a baby born with a severe cleft palate. It was their third child, and Jan found herself totally unprepared for the challenges of a special-needs child. She also admits to having very high expectations of just how much Mike was going to help her with the night feedings for the baby.

Feeding their son was an extensive ordeal requiring feeding tubes and that the baby be held in just the right position. Naturally, Jan hoped Mike would get up with her every couple of hours to help. But Mike was working full time and badly in need of *some* sleep each night in order to continue to hold the family finances together.

Because of the stress and the constant sleep loss, Jan and Mike began to blame each other for their unrelenting anxiety.

Unrealistic expectations, finger pointing, and acute fatigue opened the door to unforgiveness. Jan describes her final condition as being a "hornet's nest of bitterness."

But they both valued their marriage, and they refused to let their hard hearts undermine the foundation of their union. They eventually turned toward each other and toward God, obeying His directive to "forgive men when they sin against you."

In His mercy, the Lord washed away the bitterness and negative emotions, returning them to the contented, happy partnership they had always shared.

Symptoms of an Attitude of Unforgiveness

1. The silent treatment.

Also known as the "I'm not punishing him, I'm just not talking to him right now" treatment. I've known women who, in an effort to maintain their Christian demeanor, don't communicate with their husbands when they're angry—but instead give their husbands the silent treatment. *I'll show him how I'm feeling—by refusing to tell him how I'm feeling.*

Him: What's wrong, honey?

Her: Nothing.

Him: I can tell something's wrong—now what is it?

Her: Nothing.

Him: I can't help the problem if I don't even know what's wrong! What's wrong?

Her: Nothing.

The silent treatment can be an indicator that a woman has a rap sheet tucked in her hip pocket. Her husband's behavior has so infuriated her that she has no words left (pretty amazing for *any* woman!). Or she may feel that the silent treatment is a "just" way to penalize him for the most recent transgression. But it's a no-win situation for the poor husband, who loses if he tries to find out what's wrong—and loses if he doesn't. Either way...she's not talking. You could interrogate her for hours under a glaring spotlight in a dingy, smoke-filled room—she's *not* talking.

2. A hard heart.

He tells you he's depressed about work, and you think, *Whatever...*He tells you the doctor says his cholesterol is dangerously high, and you think, *Whatever...*He tells you he thinks he may be having a mental breakdown, and you think, *Whatever...*

The inability to care about what concerns your man is a screaming symptom that the disease of unforgiveness has caused your heart to grow cold. A woman's heart is a tender thing. In the chest of every woman—whether she's sixteen or one hundred and sixteen—beats the heart of a little girl that can be easily crushed. If she's hurt long enough, she will eventually turn her heart away and become hardened.

Although you may be tempted to harden your heart toward your husband because he repeatedly hurts your feelings, you *must* make the effort to continuously stay in an attitude of forgiveness. Remember, you won't be doing it alone. God will strengthen you. He is ready to provide the healing balm of His presence when you choose to forgive and go forward.

3. Expecting the worst.

As *another* offense is committed, you're almost glad because it's one more that can be added to an already long list. You'll pull that list out at an advantageous moment to use as proof of his continual disregard for your feelings.

An attitude of unforgiveness will set us up to expect the worst in our husbands. And when we expect the worst, it's often exactly what we get.

Expecting the worst can become like a well-traveled road—it's familiar, it's safe, and it protects us from being disappointed...again. Expecting the worst causes you to keep your expectations low (not a good thing in my book) and serves as an indicator that you are simmering in a pot of unforgiveness. Cook in it long enough, and you'll become a nit-picky, pruny puss.

A woman who expects the worst from her husband has a battle ahead of her. It's like a tree with deep roots that haven't grown overnight. It will require a complete change of heart, a desire to receive God's perspective on her husband, and forgiveness of all the past wounds inflicted upon her. She must be committed to making a fresh start with her husband—forgiving every past infraction—and beginning with a clean slate.

If you find it very difficult to forgive, today is a new beginning. Don't wait until you "feel" like forgiving; frankly, you probably never will. Instead, *decide* to forgive.

You've been robbed long enough! Can't you see the splendor of Liberty Kingdom through the lattice gate? Can't you hear the majestic voice of King Rapha bidding you entry? Now is the time to take your book of *Wounds* and fling it—with all your might—into the River of Forgetfulness.

There! Doesn't it feel good to have that heavy weight gone? Look, Sentry Clean Slate has opened the gate for you! Don't just stand there, girl—gather up your skirt and *run!*

8

The Lowdown on Lockdowns

AFTER MY ENTANGLEMENT with the pastor, I came to accept the fact that my behavior toward men needed to be radically different from my behavior with women.

Here's what I mean. I can sit right down next to a female friend...I can hug her...I can touch her hair...I can pay her a personal compliment. It is different with men. For one thing, they are visual. They are turned on by a full frontal hug. They respond physically when a woman sits down next to them on a couch, snuggled up thigh to thigh.

Song of Solomon 4:12 talks about how a married woman is to be a *locked* garden, a *sealed* fountain. That means when we're in close proximity to a man other than our husband, there should be a "lockdown" in process.

We have become careless in our current Christian culture. Sometimes we are tempted to believe that godly boundaries are based on societal implications, but that simply isn't true. Truth is *not* relative. The only plumb line for correct behavior is God's eternal Word.

Seven Important Reasons Why Our Conduct with Men Should Be Different from Our Conduct with Women

Reason #1: To honor God.

> Flee from sexual immorality. All other sins a man commits are outside his body, but he who sins sexually sins against his own body. Do you not know that your body is a temple of the Holy Spirit, who is in you, whom you have received from God? You are not your own; you were bought at a price. Therefore honor God with your body. (1 Corinthians 6:18–20)

My body is a temple of the Holy Spirit. I am filled with the very presence of Jesus Christ! When I gave my heart to the Lord almost twenty years ago, I traded my filthy rags of unrighteousness for His pure garments of salvation.

The price for these new garments? The blood of Christ Himself, shed for me and you. What a glorious truth!

Not only did I receive the amazing gift of salvation when I accepted the sacrifice of Jesus and asked Him to be Lord and King over my life, I also received the precious gift of the Holy Spirit. He dwells in me now—guiding, comforting, correcting, and enlightening. Where there used to be a self-seeking and unsatisfied woman running my life, now the King of Glory resides and presides.

But as my past behavior has indicated, I must guard my integrity and purity, working out my salvation with fear and trembling.

> Continue to work out your salvation with fear and trembling, for it is God who works in you to will and to act according to his good purpose. (Philippians 2:12–13)

Why must I continue to work out my salvation with fear and trembling? Because we're in a war. We have a very real enemy who is seeking to kill, steal, and destroy the integrity, virtuousness, and reputation of the church at large.

One way Satan accomplishes this task is by the constant assault and tearing down of Christian marriages. Each and every Christian marriage is a prize of redemption to the Lord. Each is exceedingly important to Him—a way of exemplifying His love for the church as a whole. A Christian marriage is a "showing" of the Lord, to display His love for the body of Christ.

> Husbands, love your wives, just as Christ loved the church and gave himself up for her to make her holy, cleansing her by the washing with water through the word, and to present her to himself as a radiant church, without stain or wrinkle or any other blemish, but holy and blameless....
>
> "For this reason a man will leave his father and mother and be united to his wife, and the two will become one flesh." This is a profound mystery—but I am talking about Christ and the church. (Ephesians 5:25–27, 31–32)

Just as Jesus doesn't cut us loose when we fall short, we are called to model that Christlikeness—forgiving and overlooking each other's faults and failures, resisting the temptation to cut and run when the marriage is not meeting our needs.

We need to make a determined effort to raise the bar concerning our behavior. Because of the way that men are wired, we cannot behave the same way around them as we do with women.

We are to honor God in all our relationships. When we do,

we honor not only God but also our brothers in the Lord—by not presenting ourselves to them as a temptation.

Reason #2: To honor our husbands.

> You are a garden locked up. (Song of Solomon 4:12)

Recognizing and acting upon the truth that my behavior, dress, and demeanor reflect that I am a married woman brings great honor to my husband. The above Scripture tells me that I am *his* locked garden.

Tracy considers herself a faithful wife, loving mom, and consistent Christian. On a typical day of running errands, she stops by the dry cleaners...Office Depot...the grocery store... Costco. Her only crime is the curvaceous bottom she plainly displays through the thin material of her low-rise drawstring sweatpants. The word *Pink* is embroidered on her shapely rump, and the top edge of her lacy underwear peeks out, teasing onlookers.

The fact is, Tracy doesn't look any different from her friends...or their friends. This is just how a contemporary woman dresses these days, she reasons.

Let's return to the metaphor of a locked garden. Tracy's not doing such a hot job of hiding her fruit, is she? In fact, Tracy is in full bloom: She's in great shape, vivacious, and physically attractive. She is her husband's fragrant, lovely garden. But instead of this garden being for his delight alone, her fruit is hanging over the fence, tempting onlookers to steal a piece. She's readily giving out samples to all interested males. Old men and young alike naturally find their eyes drawn to such things as the word *Pink* embroidered across a woman's curvy tush. And when a man's eyes travel down to a woman's bottom, there's a good chance that he's doing more than admiring the results of her leg lifts—more likely he's imagining her naked.

I'm not making this stuff up. It's true, and Christian women need to start acting like it's true. It is not appropriate to dress provocatively in front of any man except your husband.

Reason #3: To stay pure.

During announcements last Sunday morning, my pastor suggested we greet the people sitting around us. I turned to Tom, one of the elders at our church, and he gave me his signature "purity" hug: With his arms lightly resting upon my shoulders, he leans in as if there were an oversized balloon between us and gently pats me on the back.

Tom is effusive in his love, and is gracious and kind as he acknowledges my presence. Yet he has expressed this without embracing me. I greatly esteem a man who knows how to hug a woman without intimately touching her. Tom is a trustworthy man of honor.

But I can sure remember *other* hugs from men that weren't so wholesome. Do you remember the Looney Tunes cartoon character Pepé Le Pew, the amorous skunk, and how he falls desperately in love with the kitty in every episode? Pepé Le Pew is constantly gathering his beloved kitty in his arms, desiring to hug her, love her, and squeeze her. Kitty always has a panicked look on her face while she claws at the air, trying to free herself from Pepé's embrace. Well, I've had a few of those kinds of hugs. You know, the kind where you're practically peeling his arms away.

There are several ways to deflect a "Pepé" hug: As the skunk—er, I mean *man*—approaches, quickly turn sideways and offer the solid "side yard" of your shoulder rather than the "frontage property" of your chest.

Another way to send a skunky hugger on the run is to refuse to respond to his clingy embrace. Have you ever hugged someone who just stands there with their arms slumped to their sides (think "snotty teenager")? Use this technique in response to an unwanted embrace. Do not respond politely to a Pepé hug by putting your arms around the offender.

The last way to divert the clutching, crushing caress of a Pepé hugger is with a handshake. As Pepé approaches, arms extended for what promises to be another sticky, clingy embrace, extend your hand for a handshake. You will thereby send a clear message that you are not participating in his hands-on research project of the female anatomy.

While I cannot control the way in which a man attempts to hug me, I have control over my hugging style. I take my cue from elder Tom and do my best to "lean out" a little when hugging a man other than my husband. I used to think that this hugging rule applied to everyone except young men and old men—but time has taught me this rule applies to *all* men.

Make an effort to hug with discretion. If you find yourself pulled into a Pepé Le Pew embrace, say laughingly but firmly, "Whoa, there, fella—that's a little too tight!"

Remaining pure means guarding not only your physical self but your emotional self as well. Guarding yourself emotionally means committing to not engaging in deep, meaningful, intimate conversations with men other than your husband. Pouring your heart out to a guy can be dangerous territory.

Jennifer weathered a situation in which a female friend of hers regularly sought the advice of Jennifer's husband, Scott, for her marital problems. Sally respected Scott's opinion and wisdom, and she felt comfortable sharing her heart with him.

Over time, Sally's confidences evolved from seeking Scott's advice on general conflict to sharing intimate details about her and her husband's sex life. This was the point at which Jennifer and Scott felt the counseling sessions had run their course.

Frankly, this behavior on Sally's part is predatory. The message she sent Scott was: "I'm going to tell this big, strong, handsome man all about my private marriage problems, and he's going to try and fix them. Meanwhile, I'll be receiving some much-needed male attention, and it's all under the umbrella of 'Christian counseling.'"

I'm sure Sally didn't start off with the intention of stealing her friend Jennifer's husband. She was in emotional pain, and looking for help and comfort. Seeking counsel from a godly Christian man probably seemed like a wise solution to her marital woes; after all, she badly needed a Christian man's perspective when it came to dealing with her husband.

But seeking guidance from her friend's husband *in private* is where the trouble began. Many women are tempted to think, *I've known him for years...we're like brother and sister...I have no interest in him whatsoever...and he's my good friend's husband, after all! It's completely innocent.* Blah, blah, blah.

We must *guard* our emotional purity. What if Scott lacked integrity, didn't tell Jennifer what Sally divulged, and continued extending counsel when the conversation took an intimate turn? Eventually, Scott may have been tempted to "fix" Sally's problems by stepping in for her husband and fulfilling needs that weren't being met at home.

Intimate conversations are like a drawbridge to divorce. Sally shares with Scott about her unhappy marriage...the bridge begins to lower. She divulges private details of her sex life...the bridge lowers some more. She shares her need for attention...the bridge lands with a *thud*—and temptation beckons.

While sincere and legitimate counseling certainly holds an important place in a strained or troubled marriage, confiding in a male friend is usually not the righteous or godly way to victory. For purity's sake, we ladies should be filtering our behavior around men, keeping ourselves virtuous by holding back physical attention and emotional connection.

Reason #4: To protect the feelings of other women.

Wes and Vicki stood at the front of the church auditorium and shared the exciting details of their recent mission trip to Ecuador. As they talked, I found myself enthralled by their testimony and especially touched by Wes's sharing about the leap of faith it took for him to join an adventure like that.

Since I had to leave the Sunday service early, I decided to write a quick note to Wes, expressing my appreciation of his willingness to share his testimony. I asked a friend to deliver it and left the service.

Vickie called a short while later and told me, without mincing words, that she was upset I had written her husband a personal note. She felt it was improper and a betrayal of our friendship, and that it was inappropriate to address the note to Wes alone.

My initial reaction to her accusation was shock. However, after thinking about it for a while, I saw that she had a valid point. She had been struggling with insecurity in her marriage for some time, and my note fed the fire of suspicion.

"Wes, what a wonderful testimony you shared today! Thank you for telling us all about your amazing trip..." Vickie took one look at my note and thought, *What, am I invisible? That's funny—I thought I went to Ecuador, too!*

Vickie's call took place several years ago, and it helped change my thinking and the way I conduct myself around men who are not my husband. Her willingness to be honest, her straightforward approach, and her transparency helped raise the bar for my own behavior. I'm also grateful that she chose to confront me about the situation, rather than talking about me behind my back.

I've come to understand that flattery and compliments are heady stuff—best given out in small doses. Flattering another woman's husband may hurt *her* feelings and cause her to feel left out and insignificant. Little notes, special attention, familiarity with the opposite sex, and specific compliments are a lot like applying my favorite perfume, Jungle Gardenia: *A little goes a long way.*

Reason #5: To be a godly example to younger women.

> Abstain from all appearance of evil. (1 Thessalonians 5:22, KJV)

> Then they [the older women] can train the younger women to love their husbands and children, to be self-controlled and pure, to be busy at home, to be kind, and to be subject to their husbands, so that no one will malign the word of God. (Titus 2:4–5)

As a woman in her midforties, I am called to set an example for younger Christian women. I am called by God to instruct younger women to love their husbands deeply, to raise up godly children, and to dress and act with propriety. Setting a good example for younger Christian women is certainly not my job alone—but a responsibility of *all* Christian women.

If you are a woman in your late twenties, you must be setting an example for the girls in their late teens and early twenties. If you're in your thirties, with one baby on your hip and another in preschool, you should be setting an example for the gals in their twenties, and so on. We need to be living our lives in such a way as to mentor younger Christians.

Kathryn, our church secretary, is a lovely young woman in her midtwenties. She told me recently about how her friendship with Kathy, a "fortyish" woman from our church, has impacted her life.

According to Kathryn, Kathy initiated the friendship, reaching out to her with wisdom and a caring heart. Kathy has invited her on long walks and out to lunch—willing to share her time and willing to share herself—to make a positive impact on Kathryn's life.

Kathy is living out the admonition found in Hebrews 10:24:

> And let us consider how we may spur one another on toward love and good deeds.

It's important for us to make ourselves available to others. In addition to that, it's good for us to remember that our younger sisters in the Lord are *watching* us, and learning from our example.

In a different scenario, Sylvia throws her head back and laughs with uninhibited gaiety. Robert has just said something comical, and Sylvia is obviously amused. She playfully punches him in the bicep and tosses her long auburn hair back in that coquettish way of hers. She responds to Robert's joke with a wink and a witty retort that sets off a new round of laughter.

Sylvia and Robert have undeniable chemistry and a great relationship. The only problem is that Sylvia is married to James—the disgruntled curmudgeon waiting at the door.

If we are to "abstain from all appearance of evil," then

it's important to keep a measure of decorum in our enjoyment of the opposite sex. Younger women are learning by example how "to love their husbands, and be self-controlled and pure."

Reason #6: Not to "lead on" other men.

Many years ago I took a daily two-mile walk around my neighborhood. Each day I would encounter an elderly gentleman walking in the opposite direction. Jim and I became friendly over time, and over time we began stopping to chat for a minute or two before continuing on our separate ways.

This went on for some time. After a while, I noticed that Jim was doing his best to prolong our conversations. Hmmm…

Then I observed that Jim seemed to be dressing nicer. Hmmm…

Next, I noticed that when Jim caught sight of me coming toward him, he would quicken his step and break out in a huge smile. Hmmm…

Jim began dropping personal information about his wife and lamenting his "loveless" marriage. Hmmm…

I admit, perhaps I wasn't the quickest thirty-year-old around—but I finally caught on: Jim had a crush on me!

(*Eeeeew!* No way! Not possible!)

But yes, it was true. This eighty-year-old man from down the street was "sweet on me." And I had to ask myself, *What on earth did I do to cause him to think that I might be interested in him?*

Well, I was friendly, attentive, caring, and a good listener. In my mind, I was just being a good neighbor and taking the time to care about an elderly man in my neighborhood. In his mind, I was an attractive thirty-year-old woman who could possibly be interested in a May/December romance. While I never intended to send the wrong signals to Jim, he saw my friendliness as flirtatiousness.

After spending time in prayer, the Lord revealed to me that because Jim was crushing on me, I needed to distance myself from him.

I think my typical reaction would have been to laugh over the situation with my girlfriends and continue being kind to Jim. But I discovered that God felt much more strongly about it. Jim was a man. A very old man, but a man nonetheless. And to knowingly feed the desire of any man who is interested in you is wrong.

We are to guard our behavior toward other men because we don't know what's going on in their minds. *You* might not have any interest in that young intern at work—but *he* may be daydreaming about you morning, noon, and night. Be careful that you don't give him fodder for his fantasy. Sometimes a man can mistake kindness for romantic interest. Kindness and caring are best bestowed by you and your husband, as a couple, when it comes to giving attention to other men.

Jeff and I used to live across the street from a nice guy named Jack. He was single and didn't do too much cooking, so I would regularly take over home-cooked meals when we had leftovers. I was always careful to say things like, "Jeff and I thought you might enjoy this stew." I didn't stay long, but would drop it and go. There were clear boundary lines, and Jack never mistook my home-cooked offering as an invitation to "get cooking with him."

Because women tend to be nurturing and tenderhearted, we need to make sure that we don't coddle or "mother" other men. In other words, it is definitely possible to be *too* nice. But with clear boundaries and restrained affection, we can be sure to ward off any unwanted crushing.

Reason #7: To maintain self-respect.

Women are bombarded by conflicting messages.

On one hand, we receive an almost militant message by an Oprah-ized media to love ourselves as we are: "Respect yourself, girlfriend—acknowledge the goddess within!"

On the other hand, women are fed a steady diet of siliconed, Botoxed female role models, conveying the message that we should be looking smoother, firmer, bigger (in the right places), smaller (in the right places), and eternally young. So what's a woman to do? How's a girl to maintain self-respect in a world such as this?

> Therefore, if anyone is in Christ, he is a new creation; the old has gone, the new has come! (2 Corinthians 5:17)

Perhaps when you read my story about Tracy and her *Pink* sweats, you cringed. You may have been tempted to rationalize, "That's what all my friends wear...I can't find any sweats that aren't low-rise...I can't help it if I have a shapely figure... the pastor's wife wears sweatpants that say *Juicy* on the rear, so by comparison I'm not that bad!"

Self-respect comes from seeing yourself as God sees you, and developing a fresh perspective and improved self-image from the relationship you share with Him. The Scripture above tells us that we become a new creature when we are born again. Let's take a look at this same Scripture in the Amplified version:

> Therefore if any person is [ingrafted] in Christ (the Messiah) he is a new creation (a new creature altogether); the old [previous moral and spiritual

condition] has passed away. Behold, the fresh and new has come! (2 Corinthians 5:17, AMP)

One of the main reasons Christian women need to restrain their behavior around other men is to maintain self-respect and a modest, virtuous identity.

My identity is not discovered and realized in the admiring glances of other men, but ultimately in the fact that God's Word is true: I am a new creature *altogether*! The old immoral Paula is gone—and when she tries to rear her ugly head, I remind myself that I am a new creature in Christ. The old has *gone*...the new has *come!*

My self-respect is not garnered from the pop psychology appeal to "love myself," but rather from the day in, day out relationship I have with Christ. It is obtained as I get my nose in His Word each day...maintained as I spend time telling Him what's on my heart in prayer...sustained by hearing His still, small voice directing me.

There's a "Lockdown" in Progress

A Lockdown in Touch

Ashley, the nineteen-year-old daughter of one of my friends, just arrived home from a mission trip to Mexico.

"Ash, you look fabulous, honey!" I tell her. "Come here and let me get my hands on you." After a long squeeze I finally release her, and then run my fingers through her silky hair. "Oh Ashley, I really love your haircut...who did it?" After noticing her hair, I then comment on her deep tan while lovingly caressing her forearm. I continue to fuss over her, touch her, compliment her, and love her.

Ashley is like my own daughter, and I love her. One of the ways that I show my affection to her is by petting her hair, hugging her, noticing her great clothes, and telling her how smart and accomplished she is. She is a female, and for females, it is perfectly acceptable for us to fuss over each other. It's how we show acceptance and sisterhood. But on this front, what's good for the goose is most definitely not good for the gander.

Mike, a young man from our church, has also recently returned from a mission trip to Mongolia, and I was excited to see him. This young man is highly esteemed in my eyes, and I welcomed him home with gusto. But let me tell you, it looked a whole lot different than when Ashley returned.

I greeted him heartily. "Mike, you're home! Welcome! It's so good to see you! How are you?" I gave him a nice hug (*not* Pepé le Pew style) and a pat on the back. That was it. No lavish compliments, no flattery. Nothing like "Mike, you big, strong, handsome man, where have you been hiding yourself, Tiger?"

As women, we have every right to lovingly touch and effusively compliment the girls and women in our lives. But when it comes to guys, I'll share with you a favorite line from the movie *Moonstruck*: "Stifle yourself!"

A Lockdown in Conversation

I have in my life a variety of women: bright, loving, spiritual, caring, and funny. But it's my friends' humor and wit that I appreciate most.

And while there are occasions when we get on each other's nerves, I wouldn't trade even one of them for all the tea in China (or all the coffee in Starbucks, for that matter).

When we're at a ladies' gathering, we often get carried away with loquacious discussions and noisy laughter. For example, while in the middle of a humorous discourse on "small breasts," my friend Karen made her point by pulling up her T-shirt, revealing a quick peek at her petite, brassiere-clad bosom—eliciting more laughter and animated chatter.

We girls have also been known to have lengthy conversations about our gynecologist, Dr. Greene (in our small town there's only one), and we talk endlessly about our childbirth experiences. We discuss sex drives, menstrual cramps, stretch marks, and PMS.

We are girlfriends, and we know how to talk. That's just the nature of the beast. Conversing with each other is how we process…it's how we grow…it's how we mature. Women possess the gift of being able to be intimate in their friendships.

Even though the women that I hang with know how to have fun and are free in expressing themselves, we also know when to shut up. I was waiting in line for the bathroom at church several Sundays ago when my friend Cleo remarked to Karen (the shirt lifter) about her black underwear that was barely poking out the top of her pants. Cleo was teasing Karen, saying what a "hot mama" she was, when suddenly we noticed that a young man from our discipleship school was approaching the bathrooms. Immediately the "black panty" conversation ended.

We love our brothers in the Lord, and in no way do we want to be responsible for causing them to stumble. Rather than continue to joke about Karen's choice in underwear, we put a lid on it.

Now that's a lockdown!

A Lockdown in Intimacy

Jason needs prayer. A sudden job loss and the recent death of his father have left him with beleaguered faith and a hopeless thought life.

Laura is a compassionate friend and prayer warrior. She is moved by Jason's plight and wants to help. She begins with a warm and sympathetic hug. They find two chairs near the front of the sanctuary, and while sitting knee to knee Jason pours out his problems to her. It feels so good to finally relieve himself of his many concerns and fears, and Laura responds with heartfelt prayer and encouraging words. After they pray, Laura gives Jason one more bear hug and they part.

Hopefully at this point you are sensing the red light.

Prayer is a very, very intimate and connecting activity. I learned a long time ago that if I am going to pray with a man, I need to make the effort to include other people. Prayer is bonding, and will often involve hearing about someone's personal problems and the issues that are close to their heart.

The next week, when Jason saw Laura at church, his eyes brightened and he felt an instant connection and overflowing appreciation for her. But it would have been better for Jason to have received prayer from a man, or a small group of people. Then Jason could feel an emotional connection with a group, rather than with Laura as an individual.

A lockdown in intimacy means that I will avoid any activity (yes, even spiritual endeavors) that foster familiarity, endearment, and closeness with a man other than my husband.

A Lockdown in Compliments

Several weeks ago our family was having dinner at my friend Janet's house. She had invited her next-door neighbors, Darin and Anna, and their two lovely, curly-haired preteen daughters to join us. One of the girls walked through the kitchen where we were all visiting, and I said to the mother, "Oh Anna, your girls have such beautiful hair!"

She remarked, "Thank you! You really have beautiful hair too, Paula."

I responded, "Oh, thank you! You have absolutely great hair, Anna. What gorgeous curls you've passed on to your girls."

Then she said, "Well, thank you. And your daughter Amy has such long, pretty hair."

And on and on we went.

This is just women being women. One of the ways that women show kindness, love, and approval is to verbally compliment each other. We "fuss" over each other with our words. We do our best to notice each other's new clothes, hairstyles, and weight losses. But imagine this same scenario played out over a male visitor to Janet's house.

"Frank, how *are* you? My gosh, you handsome dog, have you been working out? I just love the way those jeans hug your physique—you've lost weight, haven't you? And that blue shirt looks so great on you. You should definitely wear more blue— it brings out the color of your eyes!"

Around the small mountain town where I live there are signs posted that read "Don't feed the bears." And when it comes to giving other men gratuitous compliments, the same advice holds true.

In fact, I want you to take a minute and think about how you felt the last time someone of the opposite sex unexpectedly tossed a compliment your way. Flushed, gratified, delighted, a little embarrassed? Perhaps you smiled, cast your eyes downward, and tucked your hair behind your ear. You may have said, "Oh stop," but what you really thought was, *Tell me more...*

Effusive compliments between men and women who are not married are like fuel for the fire of seduction. Even if it never goes any further, flattery still has the potential to draw our eyes away from the one we are married to, and it should best be avoided.

A Lockdown in Familiarity

Last weekend my daughter, Amy, and I cried and sighed our way through the movie *Pride and Prejudice*. We were lifted high on the wings of romance and transported to the lush countryside of Old World England, to a time and place where women were shy and demure and men were formal and decorous.

In that era, there was quite a contrast between the way a woman would greet another woman and the way she would greet a man. For example, when *Pride and Prejudice's* Elizabeth (played in the movie by Keira Knightley) sees her very close girlfriend Charlotte after many months, they throw themselves into each other's arms for a long embrace. There is no holding back in their affection. But later in the movie, Elizabeth has the opportunity to greet her friend Mr. Darcy— and does nothing more than curtsy.

Things are not as they once were.

Overfamiliarity between men and women who are not married breaches the line of decorum. But as I said at the beginning of this chapter, the boundary lines for godly behavior are not drawn by an irreverent and sinful society—they are drawn by God's Word. What we expect from ourselves as Christian women should be based on the Lord's requirements, and not the media's persuasion.

One important way to begin implementing God's instructions to us as wives is by attesting to the fact the no man is "safe" except our own husband—and then *acting* as if it were true.

A Temptation in Progress

Happily married and the mother of three teenagers, Heather went through an ordeal some years ago that tested what she believed about herself and what she believed about God.

Heather's church was planning a three-week mission trip to Mexico City to repair a local orphanage and sponsor several evangelistic crusades. This exciting adventure was opened up to the congregation and Heather and her husband, Stan, agreed that it would be the opportunity of a lifetime for her and the kids. Although Stan was unable to join them, he sent them with his blessing.

Twenty people from Heather's church signed up for the trip, including Hank, a married father of one. Hank's wife had work responsibilities that would keep her in the States, so he and his sixteen-year-old daughter were looking forward to the challenge and some father-daughter bonding time.

With anticipation and great excitement the group arrived in Mexico City, full of faith, full of joy, and ready to get to work. And in the unique incubator of a mission trip environment, friendships were formed and bonds made.

Heather and her three kids, along with Hank and his daughter, were assigned to the work crew that would be renovating the orphanage. Together they labored, shopped for supplies, and ate their meals. Heather and Hank soon realized that they enjoyed each other's company immensely. They made each other laugh—a powerful aphrodisiac—and each morning they began to anticipate seeing one another...perhaps a little more than they should have.

Hank complimented Heather subtly—without saying it in so many words, he let her know that he thought she was attractive. As the days wore on, Heather often caught Hank stealing glances at her. Soon the friendship took on what she began thinking of as a "sparky" quality, meaning that electricity was generated simply by their being together. Simple touch, prolonged eye contact, or just running errands—their interaction began to take on an almost "foreplay" quality.

Smashed together on a crowded Mexico City bus one day, Hank and Heather exchanged friendly banter and humorous barbs. As Heather feigned anger at one of Hank's jokes, he teased, "You're cute when you're angry..."

Later that evening Heather sat in her hotel room, buried her face in her hands, and did what she had done almost every night of that mission trip—cried out to God for help. As the Bible lay open on her lap, tears fell while she sought God with all her heart. Shame and the embarrassment of giving in to temptation threatened to paralyze her prayer life. But she pressed on.

The end of the mission trip finally came, and the group of twenty disbanded in the church parking lot after almost two days of travel. With a chaste hug and a few benign parting words, Heather bid farewell to Hank. And then she walked away with a heart *full* of regrets.

Although nothing had happened between them sexually, and no proposition had been made, Heather still felt like a battering ram had pummeled her heart and mind.

Why had she so easily let her guard down? *Why* hadn't she gone to the trip leader and request a different work detail? *Why* had she responded positively to Hank's compliments?

Heather loved her husband with all her heart. She valued her family above all earthly blessings. She knew Hank to be a man who adored his little family. They were both committed Christians and family-oriented people.

What had happened in Mexico City?

Heather told me that it was strained for a while with Hank—and she made an effort not to engage in lengthy conversations with him when she ran across him at church or social engagements. As she sought God regarding the situation, the Lord directed her to make what she referred to as "steps toward home" to fully gain emotional freedom. (I'll get to these steps in a minute.)

As you read Heather's story, did you find yourself identifying with it? It doesn't have to have been a mission trip, but any situation in which you were thrown together with a man other than your husband for a prolonged period of time. You find him attractive, he finds you attractive. He has the same sense of humor or interests as you, and you find his personality engaging. Maybe you've been working closely on an extensive project together at work, or possibly he's been doing some carpentry at your home for several weeks. Maybe the two of you have been working closely on a large fundraiser together, or planning a function for your church. It doesn't matter the situation—the point is, as you read Heather's story, your face burned. You felt as though you'd given a piece of your heart away.

In hindsight, Heather saw many ways in which she could have deflected the temptation to become too close with Hank. And we could discuss those—but in actuality, we've already covered the many ways to safeguard our marriages. The reality is, *she didn't*. She let her guard down.

The following "steps toward home" that Heather told me about are for an opposite-sex relationship that has already grown too close, a temptation in progress.

Steps Toward Home

1. Don't hide from God.

Adam and Eve's behavior in the Garden proves that when human beings sin, their instinctual response is to hide from God (as if He isn't aware of the situation already!).

Heather told me that she kept her sanity during that three-week mission trip by continuing to seek God and pour out her innermost thoughts to Him. In the midst of sin, in the midst of failure, and in the midst of temptation, Heather kept the line of communication open with the Lord. She told me that Psalm 103 was her mainstay, and that she never stopped crying out to God in the midst of the storm.

If you are caught in the enemy's snare, *do not* let shame keep you from God's saving hand. It's part of the enemy's plan to separate you from your Savior. Cry out day and night during temptation. Never stop! Even if you fail, even if you fall—fall *toward* God, not away. He loves you. He will help.

2. Reconnect with your mate.

For Heather, one of the most important steps toward home was reconnecting physically and emotionally with her husband as soon as she returned—and continuing to do so.

Heather quickly reestablished their "oneness," and this proved a vital step in closing the door to the enemy. She lavished verbal and physical love upon Stan and effectively turned her attention and focus upon the man she loved and desired.

After allowing an appetite to be built for another man's affection, Heather had to go through the process of reminding herself that the only male attention she desired was Stan's.

3. Turn from the memories.

Heather made a conscious decision not to replay the memories—the mutual compliments, the electric looks, the engaging conversations. She took steps toward home emotionally, in part by refusing to recall the details of her and Hank's time in Mexico. Remembering is a choice.

Choosing *not* to continue replaying specific memories is a powerful tool when emerging from a too-close opposite-sex friendship.

4. Recognize the counterfeit.

The devil is a liar! He offers counterfeit satisfaction while trying to steal that which is legitimately yours. You may be deluded in believing that, as a committed Christian, you won't ever be attracted to anyone other than your mate.

There's a lie floating around out there that says if you are *truly* happy in your marriage, there is no room for temptation. But that's ridiculous. Everyone falls short, and everyone undergoes temptation in some area of their lives. Like Heather, you may be very happily married when tempted with an attraction to another man.

The truth is, nothing more is happening than your being tempted. Don't read more into it. This man you are spending time with is not the love of your life (no matter what your emotions scream). The enemy is setting up a snare by offering you a counterfeit. Recognize it for what it is. You don't have to fall for it.

5. Ask for help.

Heather turned to a trusted friend for counsel, accountability, and transparency. After telling her girlfriend everything, they rebuilt hedges of protection around her marriage and talked at length about the proper response to Hank in the future. They prayed their way through the weeks following the mission trip, and Heather drew comfort from her friend's support.

6. Seek the Lord as never before.

During the weeks immediately following the mission trip, Heather took steps toward home by spending quality time in fellowship with the Lord.

Repentance, a cry for renewal, and a desire to be washed were predominant in her conversations with Him. She related to me that she took her wounded emotions to God, asking Him to heal her "self-inflicted" injuries. She prayed for Hank and his family, knowing that he, too, most likely regretted allowing a too-close friendship to form.

In the end, she told me, she beheld a facet of God's goodness that she had not fully known before: His unconditional love. She had heard about it...she had read about it...she had even taught about it in Sunday school—but she had never before experienced the length, depth, width, and breadth of it. She said, "Paula, it took my breath away!"

Heather told me that within a month or two of being home she found the sting of the memories gone. God was faithful to wash and repair her emotions. She said, "Although I would never choose to buddy up with Hank again, when I do have a conversation with him at church, or in a social setting, there is a guardedness on both our parts that was not there in Mexico." She added, "We've never spoken about what happened—and it's best that way."

As Heather related her story to me, a Scripture came to mind:

> But you are a chosen generation, a royal priesthood, a holy nation, His own special people, that you may proclaim the praises of Him who called you out of darkness into His marvelous light.... Beloved, I beg you as sojourners and pilgrims, abstain from fleshly lusts which war against the soul. (1 Peter 2:9, 11, NKJV)

Are you struggling with the truth of this Scripture right now? Perhaps you feel that you've lost perspective and cannot begin to identify with the truth that you are part of God's holy, chosen, and royal generation. But the answer lies in the rest of that Scripture quoted above: He has called you out of darkness, and into His marvelous light. He called Heather out of darkness when she felt weak and foolish, and tempted beyond escape. God is light, and it was when Heather made the choice to draw near to *Him*—when she was tempted—that He grasped her hand and pulled her from the trap. He'll do the same for you.

I want you to take from this chapter two directives. First, do your very best to implement a new level of lockdowns in your life when it comes to other men. Second, if you have failed at the first directive and are smack-dab in the middle of a temptation in progress, run back to the safety of your relationship with Christ. Refuse to be goaded by the enemy into hiding from the only One who can rescue you.

9

Fulfillment in Christ Alone

HAVE YOU EVER been *really* thirsty? The kind of thirst where your mouth dries up like cotton, you can hardly swallow, and all you can think about is getting your hands on some ice-cold, thirst quenching water?

My friend Janet and I were out walking one hot summer day. It was midafternoon and not a cloud in the sky. The heat from the sun was stifling, and we had inadvertently left the house without water. We both had very small children at the time, and as you mothers of toddlers know, if you find someone kind enough to keep an eye on the kids for a while, you must *run* for the door without looking back! In those busy days of diapers, snack time, and wiping off sticky hands, when I had the opportunity to get out of the house for some exercise, I was lucky if I remembered to put my tennis shoes on, let alone grab a water bottle.

So, off we went for our four-mile trek with no concern for the inevitable thirst that was to come. The first part of the walk was effortless; we enjoyed a flat road and a gentle breeze. But then...we rounded a bend to see a very steep incline looming before us, and I asked Janet, "Are we walking up that?"

My aerobics-instructing, fitness-guru, superfit friend said, "Sure, why not?" So up we went.

Well, even Miss Fitness was panting and sweating by the time we crested that demon hill. I have *never* been so hot and parched in my whole life! I felt almost panicked in my need to find some water. I kept thinking of that Nestea iced tea commercial where a hot, thirsty, sweaty man falls backward into a shimmering pool of sparkling blue water. I was dehydrated, perspiring profusely, red-faced, and lightheaded. I *NEEDED* water—now!

I still remember how Janet and I stood on the sidewalk that day discussing where and how we could get a drink of water. We were contemplating the idea of just knocking on a door in the neighborhood to see if anyone would give us a drink, when…the sprinklers suddenly went on in the yard we were standing right next to. "*Ch–ch–ch–ch*"—the most beautiful sound a thirsty person can hear.

Have you ever seen two grown women run through sprinklers? Well, you would have that day. We ran, we drank, and we doused ourselves in the streams of cold, invigorating water. There was shrieking, laughing, drinking, smiling, and most of all…refreshment.

We walked on. Wringing wet, our thirst completely satiated—we continued on our journey that swelteringly hot, cloudless summer day. We were deeply refreshed, thoroughly cleansed, and completely satisfied.

The Lord used that experience as a living picture of who He is in my life. *He* is the living water that satisfies the deepest longing and most ardent thirst. And He is speaking to you today. He lifts up His voice and cries out to you. Do you hear Him?

"Come, all you who are thirsty, come to the waters;
and you who have no money, come, buy and eat!"
(Isaiah 55:1)

His voice rings out with clarity, beckoning you...inviting
you. He encourages you to come and drink of His presence,
and it's not a one-time-only offer. He extends an invitation to
drink for the rest of your life! He is the Spring of Living Water,
and it's His presence that will deeply refresh you—from the
inside out. It's His presence that will satisfy; it's His presence
that you have longed for all your life. It's Him...it's *been* Him
all along.

"Why spend money on what is not bread, and your
labor on what does not satisfy? Listen, listen to me,
and eat what is good, and your soul will delight in the
richest of fare." (Isaiah 55:2)

The answer to every empty heart is Christ Jesus—the
Lord of glory. His Word is plain in its instruction not to spend
ourselves on what will not truly satisfy. He wants our souls to
be satisfied completely, to fully delight in His presence, His
promises, and His Word.

In this consumer driven culture that offers us "quick-fix
happiness" with every new technogadget, Jesus beckons us
with the promise of true contentment. But can His offer be
trusted? Or is it like everything else in this world—bound to
come up short in its promise of fulfillment?

I can answer that question with confidence: His promise of fulfillment is true. He is our Savior, Healer, Father, and
Counselor. He is our all in all. He is worthy of praise, honor,
and affection. He is the fountain of living water spoken about

in John 4:14. He's not *like* a fountain of living water; He actually *is* the water of life that will meet the deepest needs of our hearts.

A close and tangible walk with Christ is the single most important component to a protected, committed, and joyful marriage. Spending time in His presence will bring us healing and restoration. And when we embrace life as a restored, healed Christian (or one who is in the process of being healed and restored), we become easier to live with. We become more forgiving, more insightful, and more loving. As God's transforming Word enters our hearts and minds, we find it easier to trust God's plan for our marriages. "Let go and let God" becomes so much more than a catch phrase; it becomes an actuality in our lives.

Just like Janet and I made the choice to indulge in the water offered, you too will have to choose whether to get in the stream of cool, refreshing water.

On that hot, dry day in 1988, Janet and I had a choice in the matter. I first had to acknowledge my deep, aching thirst; then I had to partake of the refreshment at hand. We could have let our pride keep us from running through the sprinklers. And let's face it, it's not easy to drink from a sprinkler. There's no dignified way to go about this. You have to put your face into the powerful stream of water, open your mouth, and let the cold spray wet your whistle.

We discovered that there's no graceful way to sprinkle a little water on yourself when it comes to sprinklers. You just have to pluck up your nerve and take off running—screaming all the way! We were not dignified; we were not classy. We were like silly little girls. But we were cooled off, deeply refreshed silly little girls!

The reality of marriage is that sometimes it feels more like a desert than a refuge. The issues and troubles are real; the hurts and wounds are legitimate. But it's those very troubles that will cause us to recognize just how deeply thirsty we really are.

Discipline and Time

If I choose to drink deeply of Jesus, then I will do so by spending time reading His Word, praying, fellowshipping with Him daily, and joining with other Christians at church each week.

As I see it, two major obstacles threaten to upset this pattern. The first is discipline. I've had to work at disciplining myself to seek God each day. I don't like getting up early, but I'm always glad I did after a few minutes in God's Word (and a cup or two of coffee). By rising early to spend time with Him, I am accepting the Holy Spirit's offer to fill me with comfort, wisdom, counsel, and satisfaction. The Lord extends to us His availability and accessibility, calling to us each day, "Come, all you who are thirsty."

The second obstacle to enjoying fellowship with the Lord each day is time. In our fast-paced world, how do we find the time to pray, read God's Word, and attend church? I mean, come on—there are calls to make, e-mails to send, deadlines to meet, places to be, decisions to make…now! Time dictates, ordains, and dominates our priorities.

Time is the ruthless tyrant of busy, important people. But truth be told, *time* is actually a gift from our Creator. He has allotted each person a predetermined amount of time to spend on this earth. He deserves, and is worthy of, a quality portion of *His* gift of time.

When the Alta Dena dairy used to deliver milk to our house, my mother would skim off the cream and store it separately from the rest of the milk. We loved that cream! Mom would save it as a treat to pour over our homegrown strawberries. The cream was the best part of the milk.

Likewise, there's a portion of your day—for most people, the first part—that is the "cream" of the sixteen or so hours that you'll be awake.

The cream of your day is a sacrificial offering to God.

We don't talk about sacrificial offerings much these days. In an effort to be non-preachy and inoffensive, we are careful not to point fingers or demand too much from each other. Allow me, if you would, to talk about the "cream off the top" offering.

> Now Abel kept flocks, and Cain worked the soil. In the course of time Cain brought some of the fruits of the soil as an offering to the LORD. But Abel brought fat portions from some of the firstborn of his flock. The LORD looked with favor on Abel and his offering, but on Cain and his offering he did not look with favor. (Genesis 4:2–5)

The note in my *NIV Study Bible* sheds some light on this Scripture: "The contrast is not between an offering of plant life and an offering of animal life, but between a careless, thoughtless offering and a choice, generous offering. Motivation and heart attitude are all-important, and God looked with favor on Abel and his offering because of Abel's faith."[4]

I can only speak for myself, but an "Abel offering" means rising early (if need be) to carve out quality quiet time with the Lord; a "Cain offering" is reading the devotional that's on the back of the potty and calling that my "quiet time." An "Abel offering" costs me sleep, time, and energy; a "Cain offering" costs me almost nothing.

If I'm consistently spending a little time with the Lord while on the run, I have not given Him the cream; I've given Him skim milk. For some people, the cream of the day will be in the evening. For others, it will be first thing in the morning—or midafternoon, while the kids nap. The actual time of day is not what's important, but rather the willingness to *make* time for this endeavor.

You may wonder at this point in the book why one's walk with God is so essential to a happy, protected, joyful marriage. The reason is this: It's in our relationship with God that we become the kind of wife we long to be—and the kind of wife our husband needs us to be.

The Lord is helping me daily to become a godly woman, a more patient wife, a loving mom, a less critical friend, and a more devoted daughter. When I wake each morning and see myself reflected in the Lord's eyes, I know who I am. I am His beloved daughter, a work in progress, a thing of beauty. If I'm hoping to find my identity in anyone else's eyes, I will continually be disappointed.

As I make my way through this sometimes wonderful, sometimes difficult life, it's my relationship with Christ that gives me insight, stability, and joy. And as I make my way through this sometimes terrific, sometimes challenging marriage, it's God's Word that shines brightly on my path, helping me each step of the way. Seeking Him *must* be a priority.

I have found that there are four main things that motivate a Christian to seek God: obedience, desperation, thirst, and desire.

1. Obedience

Shortly after giving my heart to the Lord in 1986, I began to cry out in prayer regarding an overwhelming sense of fear that would often come upon me.

I would be going along fine, and all of a sudden panic and terror would hit me. I would find it difficult to breathe—I actually experienced a crushing feeling pressing down on my chest.

When I told my friends about it and asked them to pray for me, they would say, "What are you afraid of?" But I couldn't identify the cause. I wasn't afraid of any particular thing. It was just that a crushing fear would come over me, scaring me to the point of panic.

Eventually I grew terrified: The fear could come over me at any minute. I developed a fear of fear! After six months of enduring this torment, I finally cried out to God for deliverance. I lay facedown on the carpet one day and begged God for deliverance.

And He spoke to me. I did not hear an audible voice from heaven, but rather the gentle, clear voice of the Holy Spirit.

There were several things He asked me to do. First, I was to turn off the television programs I so enjoyed watching. As a new Christian, I was still filling my mind with crud-o-la, and I knew better. My conscience had twinged every time I watched certain shows, but I just kept doing it. However, that day I repented and became a whole lot pickier about my entertainment choices.

The second thing God spoke was that He wanted me to spend time in His presence each morning, reading His Word. I had known for a while that the Lord was telling me to do this, but I had not obeyed. The Holy Spirit spoke to me through many Scriptures that afternoon, including several in Deuteronomy 28.

I did business with God that day and came up off the carpet a new woman. I was free! The fear left that day, never to return.

I don't believe for a second that God gave me that spirit

of fear to coerce me into obeying. No, the spirit of fear came from the enemy. But the Lord promises in His Word that "in *all things* God works for the good of those who love him, who have been called according to his purpose" (Romans 8:28). Because He is good, He used that tormenting spirit of fear for His purposes in my life. It motivated me to seek God, and then it motivated me to obey God—and to keep obeying God.

How could I not want to love and serve the One who set me free? You see, it wasn't "I'm scared of God, so I had better obey." It was more, "I love my Liberator so much, how could I not seek and obey Him?"

That incident taught me the reality of James 4:7:

Submit yourselves, then, to God. Resist the devil, and he will flee from you.

2. Desperation

New Year's Eve blew in with a monstrous winter storm, and we woke up on the first morning of 2006 to several feet of fresh snow. But our delight was short-lived as news spread throughout our community that a much-loved woman and her daughter from our church had disappeared overnight in the snowstorm.

Apparently the women had attempted to take a shortcut home in the blizzard and gotten lost, eventually becoming stuck in deep snow miles from the main highway. As the snow continued to fall, their white SUV grew buried. Worse, it was hidden from the road by a canopy of trees, and set back on a steep, seldom traveled canyon road.

The people of our church and community were frantic to start searching, but first had to spend most of New Year's Day digging out their own cars and snowmobiles. Late that afternoon, the search and rescue operation finally got underway.

Early the next morning many men, women, and teenagers had been mobilized to comb the numerous mountain roads in the area. There were people searching on snowshoes and skis, in every form of snow vehicle, and in helicopters and airplanes.

Three days after becoming lost, the car was finally located by a helicopter pilot, who spotted a woman standing on top of a car, waving her hands. Unable to land, he notified the search and rescue team on the ground with her location. The entire community rejoiced to learn that she had been found, and we all made the assumption that her nineteen-year-old daughter was safely in the car with her.

But when the rescuing snowmobile finally reached the woman, it was discovered that her daughter had decided to walk out and find help. The mother had done everything in her power to stop her, but the daughter felt it was the best thing to do. She had left the stranded vehicle and her mother the previous morning.

At that point the search intensified. Every available search and rescue person was put to work. My son, Andrew, was home from college for winter break, and since the young woman was a former neighbor, friend, and schoolmate of his, he asked if he could join in the search. Andrew was instructed to stay away from the avalanche-prone mountainside where the experts were searching, and was asked to probe the deep snow on the side of the road that the car had originally traveled.

On a brilliantly sunny Friday morning that first week of January, my nineteen-year-old son found the body of his friend.

I received a call from the search and rescue trailhead team

telling me that the young woman's body had been found—and that it was my son who found her. It was suggested that I come to the trailhead to be with him.

Twenty minutes later I pulled into the staging area, just as my husband drove in from the opposite direction. As we waited for the search and rescue team to transport Andrew down the mountain, I looked up at the majestic peaks and once again relinquished my son into the hands of the living God. He may be a fully grown, independent young man, but in my heart he's still my little boy.

I was grief-stricken and crushed. Crushed for the family of that beautiful and talented young woman...crushed for the many who held out hope that she would be found alive...and crushed for my son, who never expected to confront the death of a friend in such a close and tangible way.

I have never prayed as much as I did that week. I literally cried out to God day and night for that mother and daughter. Everyone did. They were constantly in our prayers. Sleep was hard, laughter impossible, enjoyment inappropriate.

Yet in the midst of trial and suffering, I felt the nearness of God as *never* before. Even on that crisp, sunny morning as I waited for my son to come down that mountain, I felt His comforting touch.

Desperate circumstances call for desperate prayer. Desperation is often a catalyst used by God to get self-sufficient people to seek Him. Really, it's not because we need God more when we're desperate; we simply recognize our need for Him more. A difficult marriage, a wayward child, addiction, sickness, and other trials are like a ladder to heaven—they are generally the rungs that carry us up to the throne of God.

We climb the rungs of desperation and approach our heavenly Father with nothing to offer except frantic need. We empty ourselves before Him in prayer, and we come down the ladder changed. We are changed in His presence, and we depart a fiery trial different than we entered it.

Think about it: How can you spend time before the Lord and *not* be changed? How can you receive the comfort of His presence, His healing touch, His answer to prayer, His voice in the midst of the storm—and *not* be changed?

If you're in the midst of a desperately unhappy marriage, I pray that you will let the unhappiness you feel be the very catalyst that propels you toward the throne of God. I've said it before, but it bears repeating: Nothing is too difficult for God! Carry the heavy load of your troubles to Him, and lay them at His feet. Seek Him for insight. Seek Him for a prayer strategy. Seek Him for peace in *your* storm.

3. Thirst

In C. S. Lewis's *The Silver Chair*, a young girl named Jill finds herself carried into an unknown land. She is lost and extremely thirsty, and is searching for a stream. She finds a brook, but she also finds the lion, Aslan (a symbol of Christ), lying beside it. Aslan growls and tells her she may come and drink.

> "May I...could I...would you mind going away while I [drink]?" said Jill.
>
> The Lion answered this only by a look and a very low growl. And as Jill gazed at its motionless bulk, she realized that she might as well have asked the whole mountain to move aside for her convenience.
>
> The delicious rippling noise of the stream was driving her nearly frantic.
>
> "Do you promise not to—do anything to me, if I do come?" said Jill.

"I make no promise," said the Lion.

Jill was so thirsty now that, without noticing it, she had come a step nearer.

"*Do* you eat girls?" she said.

"I have swallowed up girls and boys, women and men, kings and emperors, cities and realms," said the Lion. It didn't say this as if it were boasting, nor as if it were sorry, nor as if it were angry. It just said it.

"I daren't come and drink," said Jill.

"Then you will die of thirst," said the Lion.

"Oh dear!" said Jill, coming another step nearer. "I suppose I must go and look for another stream then."

"There is no other stream," said the Lion.[5]

And that is the crux of it all, isn't it? There is no other stream by which we may drink and be satisfied. The Lion of Judah *is* the only stream. And He will not leave us unchanged if we dare to approach.

In the words of C. S. Lewis, "Aslan is not safe, but he is good." I have found my relationship with Christ to be anything but "safe," but I have found Him to be exceedingly good. It makes me think of a Scripture found in Jeremiah 2:13:

My people have committed two sins: They have forsaken me, the spring of living water, and have dug their own cisterns, broken cisterns that cannot hold water.

Because we often see a sold-out relationship with Jesus as unsafe ("Who knows what He'll do to me, or with me, if I were to give Him my *whole* life and my *whole* heart?"), we dig our own cisterns of refreshment. We might even sprinkle a little Jesus in the cistern to legitimize our endeavor. Most of the time these handmade cisterns are actually good things. Sometimes they are blessings *from* God that have become idols, and are now taking the place *of* God. These things may include:

- A career
- A ministry
- Love interest
- Food
- Recreation
- Entertainment

I did a little research and discovered that a biblical cistern was an artificial reservoir for storing water. Before 1200 BC, cisterns were dug out of the soft limestone rock found in Palestine. Because of the porous nature of limestone, these cisterns often broke and became inadequate for holding rainwater.

Another interesting fact about water collection in biblical days was that the rainwater was often collected from the roof of a home by having it run through a series of conduits until it arrived at the family cistern. You can imagine that the water wasn't very clean by the time it got to the cistern.

In Jeremiah 2:13, the Lord is convicting us of two sins. First, that we are *not* drinking from His presence enough; second, that we may be drinking stagnant, dirty water from cisterns of our own making. But in these troubling times of terrorist attacks, pandemics, famines, wars, cancer, and global warming, cistern water will never sustain or refresh us. Fear, sin, and darkness will overtake us if we aren't revitalized and cleansed daily by the washing of the water of the Word of God.

I enjoy walking on a long country road a few miles from my home. Along this rural road there are aspen trees, mountain vistas, and the runoff from several high elevation streams.

When these mountain streams overflow, the water runs in rivulets along the road, eventually becoming motionless and moss filled. What starts out as a vibrant, rushing creek dribbles to a stagnant, smelly culvert of water sitting along the side of the road.

If I were a hot and thirsty traveler I might think that the stagnant water was the only available source of refreshment. I guess I *could* drink it, but it sure wouldn't taste good—nor would it be good for me.

But to the person who is familiar with the area, drinking that stagnant water would be unthinkable! All one would have to do to find a clean, sparkling mountain stream would be to veer off the road a little and hike up a scenic trail for half a mile.

It's one thing to hear about a beautiful rushing stream in the mountains; it's another thing entirely to expend the energy to find one yourself.

If while you've been reading this chapter, you realize that you *are* thirsty for more of God, you have a choice to make. Either you can let your thirst drive you to search for the spring of living water, or you can relieve that sense of spiritual thirst by continuing to be satisfied at the usual stagnant cisterns.

My life with God has been a series of choices, most of them small, daily choices. But it is the small, seemingly insignificant choices that have actually determined the course of my life. God has a good plan for me—but I have to choose daily to obey Him *in the small things* to see His plan for me fulfilled.

The most important choice I can make is whether I will expend the energy to climb the mountain to the river of living water. My flesh wants to take the easy way, drinking from the easily accessible stagnant stream that's close by—for me, that might be television. But the inward man longs for the fulfillment and refreshment that only time spent each day with Jesus can bring.

4. Desire

Hope deferred makes the heart sick, but a longing fulfilled is a tree of life. (Proverbs 13:12)

The Lord will often use our desire for something or someone to draw us close to Him. As we seek Him, asking Him to fulfill the desires of our hearts, we find ourselves transformed by His presence—and many times our desires are transformed as well.

Three desires that in years past I often took to God in prayer were for my husband to become a Christian, for a second child, and to fulfill my call to ministry. That was many, many years ago—but those three desires kept me close to God.

Maybe you're an idealist who would hope that just plain old obedience and love for God would be the defining motivator when it comes to walking with the Lord in diligence. I like the thought of that too! But I have to tell you that a continuous motivator in seeking God was the perpetuation of these desires, which were near and dear to my heart.

I know that only He can fulfill my desires. I take comfort in the thought that God loves me dearly. The things that are important to me are important to Him. And if I get my priorities out of whack or develop a desire that is not fitting for a child of God, He will deal with me. Why? Because He loves me.

He loves you too! You are important to Him; you are the apple of His eye. What matters to you matters to Him. You will not have to twist His arm to "get what you want" out of God. Like a loving parent, He delights to give you the desires of your heart. As a new Christian, I remember my joy at finding Psalm 37:4:

> Delight yourself in the LORD and he will give you the desires of your heart.

When I read that text, I couldn't believe my eyes! Could it be possible that the Lord was directing me to "delight myself in Him" and He would do the rest? I thought, *Well, I can do that!*

So I busied myself delighting in Him. I told Him all about my desires...I poured out my heart to Him regarding my husband...I let Him know how much I wanted a little girl...I regularly prayed about my ministry. But most of all, I just got busy delighting myself in Him. Singing to Him. Reading about Him in the Bible. Talking to Him. Thanking Him. Spending time with Him. Including Him in my everyday life. And soon it became my joy to delight myself in the Lord.

Do you know what happened while I was delighting myself in the Lord? *He gave me the desires of my heart!*

I became the living, breathing admonition found in Psalm 5:3:

> In the morning, O LORD, you hear my voice; in the morning I lay my requests before you and wait in expectation.

I think sometimes we feel foolish or weak admitting that it takes a crisis or a deep, unmet longing to drive us near to God. But we must know that it's all in His plan. He knows we're just His kids. I like to come to Him as a child without everything figured out. I've learned to assume He is good. I don't try any-more to wrap my mind around His ways. I just come to Him as His child, asking for what I want and need.

If I'm seeking Him with a wrong request, He will correct me (and believe me, He has). He has also rebuked me when I've gotten too focused on my own needs, and reminded me simply to delight myself in Him.

Enjoying Jesus is one of the greatest lessons of my life. It is one that will surround me, like a beautiful fragrance, all the way to my last breath here on earth.

First Love Beckons

I stood in the moonlit parking lot outside of a condominium on a warm summer's night at 2:00 a.m. The object of my de-sire was sound asleep, I was sure, in his bedroom two floors above the spot where I held my "love vigil." I was not there to see him, nor was I there to talk to him—I only wanted to be near him. His name was Jeff Friedrichsen and I was madly, passionately in love...the kind of love that takes the place of eating, sleeping, and even rational thinking.

Jeff and I had been dating seriously for several months, and it was becoming increasingly clear to me that this was the man I would marry. I loved his voice...his stories...his wis-dom. I loved the way he walked, the way he looked, and the way he moved. I was seriously smitten, and in my youthful and romantic ardor I could not bear to be away from him. So, unable to sleep for thinking of him, I made my way through the quiet streets of our small slumbering town to stand be-neath his window and dream.

Although this experience happened well over twenty years

ago, I still remember the breathless joy of "first love."

This is the passionate response of a woman in love, and it is the same desire that our God longs for in the hearts of His children. The Lord is beckoning us to return to Him, our first love, recalling the sweet beginnings of our salvation experience. He summons us with the promise of peace, joy, righteousness, unconditional love, correction, guidance, and fulfillment. All we must do is drink.

> "It is done. I am the Alpha and the Omega, the Beginning and the End. To him who is thirsty I will give to drink without cost from the spring of the water of life." (Revelation 21:6)

While the many insights and suggestions found in this book will be helpful in your quest for a wonderful, fulfilling marriage, the most important nugget of truth is found here at the end. Press into your relationship with Christ, and the rest will truly fall into place. Put God first, husband second, children third, extended family next, and everything else after. With those priorities, you cannot and will not fail.

It's in that place of intimacy with Christ that hope begins to come alive. It's during prayer that the Holy Spirit whispers His promises for marriage. It's in God's holy Word that great and profound encouragement will bolster your sagging faith. Everything good begins with our walk with God—*especially* a good marriage!

10

Feelings Follow Action

WOMEN, AS A RULE, are more emotionally driven than men. We tend to rely upon our intuition—our "emotional barometer"—to navigate our way through life.

I believe emotions can be an important tool in dealing with troubling situations and/or people. But emotions can also mislead and misguide us. For example, if a woman is feeling terribly unhappy and bankrupt in her marriage, her emotions are not a stable or solid indicator of what action she should take to rectify her problems. Her natural tendency might be to close the door to her heart in the hopes of guarding herself from future hurt. But that may be the complete opposite of the Holy Spirit's leading.

It's always going to be best to put emotions aside and seek God for His direction and guidance regarding a troubled marriage.

Don't Put the Cart Before the Horse

Feelings follow actions, not the other way around. All too often, we *plan* to act a certain way once we genuinely *feel* that way. We say things like, "As soon as God restores the passion and love that I once felt for my husband, I'll act lovingly and passionately toward him."

But the truth is, our feelings will follow the actions we take. If I wanted to lead a mule, I would grasp the lead rope that's attached to the harness and pull; the mule would follow. I could not successfully move the mule by standing next to it and saying, "Move!" I could not move the mule by wishing it would move. I could not move the mule by praying it would move. There's an action needed.

Action will lead; feelings will follow. When we determine to turn our hearts, minds, and bodies toward our husbands, submitting our anxiety and fear of disappointment to God, we can expect our feelings to line up with our behavior.

Let's say, for example, that you choose to act respectfully toward your husband even though some of his past decisions have perhaps eroded that respect. Day in and day out you resist the temptation to bring up his past mistakes; instead, you choose to treat him with kindness and respect. At some point, your feelings will catch up with your actions, and you will begin to experience respect for your husband. Here are a few examples:

1. You choose to act lovingly toward your husband even though you aren't getting along great these days. You make it a point to say loving words, make his favorite dinners, and respect his decisions. As you do these things, somewhere along the way you begin to experience renewed love for this man. You have been reminded why you married him in the first place.

2. You choose to act happy to see your husband at the end of the day, even though upsetting circumstances at work or at home have been mentally and emotionally draining. You

make a determined effort to lay aside your frustration and display happiness at seeing him at day's end. By purposing to enjoy your husband, your emotions are soon engaged; you take comfort in his presence.

3. You choose to make yourself sexually available to your husband even though you're deeply fatigued from looking after small children all day and are not in the mood. Instead of wasting ten minutes making excuses and telling your husband how tired you are, you spend those ten minutes lavishing sexual attention upon him. Before you know it, your feelings catch up. And by evening's end, it turns out to have been a great idea!

4. You choose to be cheerful and lively around your family even though you're feeling grumpy and out of sorts. By making an effort to act pleasant and refusing to give in to that "dark cloud" feeling, you dictate the direction your stubborn emotions are to go. Soon you find yourself laughing at your children's antics at the breakfast table and joking with your husband about the burnt toast.

As you prayerfully make an effort to take the appropriate actions, your feelings will follow. Start off by acting cheerful; you'll soon find yourself feeling cheerful. Start off by acting lovingly; you'll find yourself feeling love for your guy. Start off by acting sexually available; you'll soon find yourself immersed in the pleasure of sexual intimacy with your wonderful husband. Like a stubborn mule that doesn't want to move, your emotions will be tugged along by your actions until they are galloping dutifully behind.

When I teach this principle at women's retreats, I am occasionally approached by women who say, "Paula, I'm not going to *pretend* to love him if I don't feel love for him. I'm not a liar. If I'm not happy in this marriage, I refuse to play make-believe!"

I firmly believe that having a self-important attitude prevents a woman from taking loving action toward her mate. To believe that you cannot act a certain way until you feel that way is incorrect—and it allows your emotions to dictate your life.

Please don't misunderstand me. I'm not talking about pretending to be an ever smiling, perfectly coiffed, apron clad, Stepford-like wife who never discusses her personal grievances with her husband. On the contrary—communication is of prime importance in marriage, and one we'll be discussing later in the chapter.

What I am saying is that you are in charge of your emotions, and you get to choose how you will act and even how you will feel. Your fragile, frenzied feelings aren't in charge. The godly woman inside of you—the one who desires to honor God with her life and marriage—is in charge! We aren't to be blown and tossed here and there by our ever changing feelings; instead, we are to be purposeful in our actions.

Consistently positive actions produce consistently positive feelings.

Bon Jovi's Home!

We have a little dog named Sweet Pea that we rescued from a dog shelter eight years ago. She is the most grateful, loving dog you will ever meet. After being gone for a few hours yesterday, I arrived home to my usual greeting: acrobatic spins and circus flips, followed by Sweet Pea running at full speed from one end of the house to the other, over and over again.

Now *that's* a homecoming! Whether I'm gone twenty minutes or several days, every time I come home it's the same—I am treated like a rock star by my dog. The electrified fans at a Bon Jovi concert could not be more adoring than my little Sweet Pea.

Her spirited reception yesterday made me painfully aware of my ho-hum attitude of late. It was the second week of a horrible head cold, winter seemed to be lasting forever, and lately I'd been finding it difficult to get enthused about anything. In fact, Jeff has been arriving home from work to a blasé and monotone "Hi" from the kitchen each night.

Now don't get me wrong. I don't think I necessarily need to give Jeff the "rock star" treatment. But I could probably muster a bit more than a slow blink and a monosyllabic greeting.

Determined to do better, last night I met Jeff at the door with a big hug and kiss. As I tucked my head into his shoulder, I inhaled his aftershave and remembered how glad I was to see him. I stood back and smiled, took his lunch box from him, and asked him about his day. I fought the temptation to tell him about another long day with my miserable head cold, how weary I was of the winter weather, and my upsetting website problems.

Before I walked to the front door to greet my husband, I was not feeling loving, kind, or affable. But I was determined to make the choice to get over myself and my problems, and to give Jeff some much-needed attention. And as I *acted* loving, kind, and affable, I began to *feel* that way. Why? You already know—because feelings follow actions.

The Truth About Divorce

Thomas and Emma were married in a lovely outdoor ceremony: she in a flowing white gown, he in a tailored black tux.

They began their life together with the absolute surety that they would make each other profoundly happy.

Somewhere around year two, Emma figured out that Thomas wasn't the dispenser of love elixir that she thought he was; it no longer seemed likely that he would be making her profoundly happy 24/7.

Six years of marriage and three children later, Emma decided that Thomas actually made her *un*happy. And by their tenth year of marriage, Emma reached the conclusion that Thomas made her *profoundly* unhappy.

Now, Thomas and Emma live in a comfortable home, have healthy and happy kids, are fit and active, and belong to a wonderful church. They have profitable jobs, a loving extended family, leisure time, and close friends.

What don't they have? Well, with all their material and physical needs taken care of, they have only one major complaint: They just don't make each other happy anymore. In fact, they make each other decidedly unhappy.

Arguments, betrayal, discord, angry words, disrespect, and other hurts piled up year after year. Although neither Thomas nor Emma ever intended to divorce, that's where their marriage is headed. In some ways they feel almost helpless to halt the downward spiral. Like so many other couples these days, they seem destined to wind up in divorce court.

People have always been tempted to trade partners when the going gets tough. Many have been deceived into thinking that their marital disagreements are insurmountable and hopeless; who can expect to stand under the demonic onslaught? Every individual who is going through a hard time in their marriage is certain of this: "Nobody can possibly understand the depths of my unhappiness!"

The subject of divorce is addressed often in the Bible:

"I hate divorce," says the LORD God of Israel, "and I hate a man's covering himself with violence as well as with his garment," says the LORD Almighty. So guard yourself in your spirit, and do not break faith. (Malachi 2:16)

Some Pharisees came to him to test him. They asked, "Is it lawful for a man to divorce his wife for any and every reason?"

"Haven't you read," he replied, "that at the beginning the Creator 'made them male and female,' and said, 'For this reason a man will leave his father and mother and be united to his wife, and the two will become one flesh'? So they are no longer two, but one. Therefore what God has joined together, let man not separate." (Matthew 19:3–6)

And if a woman has a husband who is not a believer and he is willing to live with her, she must not divorce him. (1 Corinthians 7:13)

God's Word plainly tells us *not* to forsake the marriage covenant. Not only because it's not in our best interests, but—equally important—because it grieves God's heart greatly and He hates it.

This is not to say that divorce is an unforgivable sin. For goodness' sake, it's not! But the Lord tells us not to do it because divorce hurts everyone involved. Divorce hurts God. Divorce hurts children. Divorce hurts the extended family. Divorce hurts the reputation of Christians. It is a trail of tears and pain that goes on for years and years—and it is the children who suffer deepest from it. It should not be an option except in extreme cases (for example, substance abuse, on-going unrepentant sexual sin, and physical or verbal abuse).

I believe that the collective cry of children of divorcees has reached the ears of God. He sees each little boy who cries himself to sleep at night because of the breakup of his family. He hears the sobs of every little girl who feels her world is falling apart because of her parents' separation. With all my heart, I believe that God is going to respond to these cries by turning the hearts of Christian married couples back to each other and back to Himself.

In the midst of the flood of divorces that are brutalizing the church and her reputation, God is raising up the standard of His Word. He is calling His people to be separate from the world, and to come out from among them. And this is done one married couple at a time.

This means that you, my friend, must stand strong for your marriage. The women who you talk to, fellowship with, or minister to—these are the women you must encourage to fight for their marriages.

As a society, we've believed the startling statistic that divorce is inevitable for at least half of the marriages, Christian or not. But an article written by Jim Killam for *Christianity Today International* shows that the 50 percent statistic is incorrect and misleading; the number of marriages ending in divorce is closer to half of that. He states:

Half of all marriages end in divorce. We know this to be true because people tell us. The media report it. Your pastor might preach it. Your friends talk about it. As one expert puts it, the statistic has become "part of American folklore."

But it's a lie. Repeat after me: Fifty percent of all marriages do not end in divorce.

If it's untrue, why won't that flawed statistic go away? Because, truth be told, no one can come up with the right statistic.

Recent research suggests that one marriage in four is closer to the true divorce rate. The 50 percent myth originated a couple of decades ago when someone looked at marriage and divorce numbers reported by the National Center for Health Statistics. The number of divorces in one year was precisely half the number of marriages. Voilà! Half of all marriages end in divorce. Right? Nope.

With this kind of math, we also could reason that everyone born this year also will die this year. After all, the number of births each year roughly equals the number of deaths. The flawed reasoning is obvious: A lot of people are alive who neither were born nor died this year. You very likely are one of them. Similarly, the divorce statisticians forgot to figure in the marriages already in existence, of which there are, oh, tens of millions.

"The media, frankly, tend to use a lot of information without ever challenging what they use," says researcher George Barna, author of *The Future of the American Family* (Moody). So the media can shoulder much of the blame for propagating an inaccurate statistic. But why don't more people challenge it?

"Many people have a vested interest in accepting it as fact," Barna says. "Preachers use it to awaken people in their churches as to how bad things are. Those who have been through a divorce may use it to rationalize what they personally have experienced. And, from a spiritual perspective, the lie is always more intriguing than the truth."

But is it a lie? Or just one of many ways to interpret the figures?

"In one sense it is true," says Scott Richert, assistant editor of *The Family in America*, a journal published by the Rockford Institute. "If you look at all marriages that took place last year, about 45 to 50 percent will eventually end in divorce." He draws that conclusion based on the fact that the annual ratio of divorces-to-marriages has been about one in two for more than a generation.

"There's been a slight downward trend in the past several years," Richert says, "but basically that number has been consistent since no-fault divorce began in 1970."

But remember, we're talking about two groups of people. Richert's statement doesn't necessarily contradict Barna's, because Richert is talking about new marriages and Barna is talking about all marriages. Among the 55-and-older population, for example, marriages are quite stable. Most marriages that fail do so before the partners reach their mid-40s. Barna's research may be the best recent attempt at finding the true divorce rate in America. His group surveyed 3,142 randomly selected adults and found that 24 percent of adults who have been married also have been divorced. The survey's margin of error is plus or minus 1 to 2 percent.

"It's (the 50% divorce statistic) a very misleading statistic and very dangerous. It contributes to a mindset in our culture that divorce is inevitable. And it may have become a self-fulfilling prophecy."

The result, Mattox believes, is disrespect for the institution of marriage. Couples casually decide to try this marriage thing for a while, and if it doesn't work out, no problem. We only had a 50/50 chance going in, right?

"Someone who enters into the institution with that kind of regard for it is much more likely, when a crisis comes along, to think, 'time to bail,'" Mattox says.

So, America, we have a problem. We also have some ammunition. Go out and challenge the one-in-two doomsayers with the truth. Tell your friends. Tell your pastor. But do it with compassion for the 24 percent, or whatever the actual number is, who have divorced. As Mattox points out, divorce still carries a certain amount of societal shame, especially for Christians. And yet, telling people that three of every four marriages won't end in divorce sure lifts some of the gloom and doom. "To me," Mattox says, "that puts things in a better perspective. It should offer people more hope."[6]

We Must Fight for Marriages!

Making a conscious decision to revel in your husband, recalling the many reasons you married him, is a wonderful first step in the process of guarding your marriage. But ultimately—even in very stable and happy marriages—there will be times when you must be willing to fight for your marriage.

Marriage must be valued by Christians. I think sometimes we women pussyfoot around the issue of divorce, in an effort to guard each other's feelings. And I hate hurting other's feelings just as much as you do—but not to the detriment of marriages. I value marriage deeply, and so must you.

Think about something you value deeply. If you're a mom, I want you to think about how much you value your children. If your house were on fire, you would risk life and limb to rescue your child. If someone tried to abduct your child, you would fight to the death to protect them. You would give anything to save the life of your child. You would fight any foe to protect him.

What you love and value, you protect. What you love and value, you fight for. Let's look at five ways in which we can love, value, and fight for our marriages.

1. Fight for your marriage with clear communication.

Helen is quiet by nature. Never a big talker, she finds it difficult to put her thoughts and emotions into words. Because of this, issues and complaints tend to build up between her and her husband, Bob. By the time she gets around to communicating with him, her bitter words spew like hot lava from an erupting volcano. Every irritating, hurtful thing that Bob has done for the last four years comes rushing forth in a scorching flow of complaints.

Communication is key in marriage because without it, the garbage never gets dumped. Yesterday a few coffee grounds, two banana peels, and an overripe cantaloupe sat rotting in the bottom of the kitchen trash can, and it began to smell. Add to that last night's chicken bones, some leftover pasta salad, and the empty cat food can, and it's becoming quite malodorous. Because it's getting full, we smash down the contents and add today's trash: orange peels, egg shells, two empty (albeit fragrant) tuna cans, and some garlic salsa that's seen better days. The trash receptacle is overflowing and putrid—and the question begging to be answered is, "Why won't someone take out the trash?"

Ongoing grievances, complaints, and annoyances need to be discussed or they build up like smelly trash. Now, some irritations should just be overlooked. (Remember, overlooking someone's faults is like looking over the top of the irritation to see the one you love standing on the other side of it.) Not everything that bothers you needs to be spoken about. But when the complaint is ongoing and is hurting your marriage, that's the time to discuss it. By stuffing your hurts and annoyances and refusing to talk about them, you are endangering your marriage.

Some women stay quiet about their complaints in a misguided attempt to display godly behavior. But their dour expressions and pursed lips are a dead giveaway as to what's going on in the inner woman. Clear communication, and even the conflict that sometimes follows, is not bad or wrong or sinful.

In my marriage of twenty-plus years, we've seldom had change or resolution *without* conflict. But because things are being regularly discussed, the garbage doesn't build up, and it's not a conflict of volcanic proportions.

2. Fight for your marriage by stepping away from the fray.

In Thomas and Nanette Kinkade's beautiful little book *The Many Loves of Marriage*, I found a lovely nugget of truth that will be helpful in the fight to guard marriages. In the chapter titled "A Sheltering Love," Thomas writes:

> For so many of the people I talk to, home isn't a refuge at all; it's just another battle zone, full of noise, confusion, and even hostility.

The TV blares away in the living room, the phone rings incessantly, and the laser blasts and planetary explosions erupt from a computer game down the hall.

Though you may not be able to control all of the factors that bring tension and confusion into your home environment, you can certainly control those. As I've mentioned, we don't include television in our home. From day one, the kids have found alternative, quieter ways to amuse themselves.

Another simple thing we do is to keep our phone on "no ring" mode at night. When someone calls, the answering machine automatically answers. As a result, we don't have to share our mealtimes or precious family moments with those seeking to drop in unannounced via telephone. Our kids' friends know this and have learned to make all their arrangements and contacts during the day. We've made it very evident to friends, extended family, and business associates that we simply don't take calls at night. Period. If it isn't life or death, it can wait until the next day.

Just eliminating those two sources of noise and confusion—the phone and the TV—makes a monumental difference. It's quiet. It's peaceful. You can hear laughter and chatter through the walls.

Withdrawing from the world, you say? Becoming insulated and exclusive, you frown? Yes. And why not? Why not savor our own little world of kindness, beauty, laughter, light, and love? Why conform to arbitrary cultural norms that steal our time and quench our joy? What can the world offer us better than what we offer each other?

The tyranny of the urgent, the pressure of a

thousand demands from numberless sources, simply overpowers the simplicity of truly important things. So we have made some choices—not as radical as they might seem on the surface—to shelter and protect our marriage and home life.

And we've never regretted it.

We're one of those rarities in the twenty-first century...a happily married couple.[7]

3. Fight for your marriage with persevering prayer.

"Nothing is too hard for you." (Jeremiah 32:17)

One of the most important ways to fight for your marriage is by faith-filled, persevering prayer. It actually takes more effort to pray in doubt than to pray in faith. To pray in doubt, you must constantly conjure up thoughts about what's going to go wrong next. To pray in faith, you simply come to God as a child, believing that He loves you and will help your marriage.

Many years ago we purchased an older home with some pretty profound battle scars. In fact, at the time of our purchase, the home was so smelly and rank that when we brought our four-year-old son to take a look at it, he had to keep running out of the house to breathe in fresh air. He would dart into the house, take a quick look around, and then lunge out the door into the front yard, sucking in great gulps of clean air.

Needless to say, we had to gut the entire house and start from scratch, putting in all new appliances, carpet, paint, and window coverings. And once the inside of the house was completely refurbished, we then turned our attention to the outside of the home. The front yard was blessed with mature shade trees, weed-free grass, and blooming rosebushes, but the fenced backyard was an absolute pit. No one had ever taken the time to plant anything back there.

That backyard became my obsession. I was determined to make it a flourishing paradise. So I got busy planting. I mixed in bags and bags of topsoil, and planted everything from grass to flowers.

Finally, I planted green bean seeds that I had decided would help camouflage the chain link fence at the back of the yard. I carefully followed the directions on the packet of the green bean seeds, poking them into the ground several inches deep. And then I waited.

Because I'm not very good at waiting, it seemed like it took forever for the green bean sprouts to show themselves. The instructions stated it would take two weeks for the green beans to sprout. So at exactly two weeks and one day, I gave up on the seeds, assuming they were duds, and took off for the nursery to buy some honeysuckle plants.

Pushed on by my manic desire to transform my backyard into a flourishing garden paradise, I set about planting the honeysuckle in the same location I had planted the green bean seeds. Since I had completely given up on those green beans, I wasn't even looking for signs of life in the soil while digging my new holes for the little honeysuckle plants. I still remember kneeling in the dirt that day, and to my shock finding a green bean seed, split wide open, with a two-inch sprout just about ready to poke through the soil. I had given up on something that was within hours of bursting through the darkness.

That was the day the Lord opened my eyes to the fact that things are not always as they appear. As I looked upon that sprouted green bean seed, God made it clear to me that my long buried seeds of prayer would come to fruition someday. He showed me that the secret hopes and desires of my heart—those things hidden from the light of day—would sprout into being at the proper time. My responsibility was to keep praying (plant seeds of prayer), keep trusting (water them with faith), and not lose heart. It was God's job to make my seeds of prayer grow into the desired results.

Many years have since passed, and we eventually moved from that house. Although my backyard never did quite become the paradise of my imagination, it did become a cool and shady yard for my son to play in. The green bean plants grew strong and tall, covering the ugly chain-link fence (they even produced a few emaciated green beans).

But the most important thing that came from that experience was the lesson of hope. We can never give up on our prayers. God is listening. At just the right time, in just the right season, He will bring the harvest.

Let us not become weary in doing good, for at the proper time we will reap a harvest if we do not give up. (Galatians 6:9)

4. Fight for your marriage with the words of your mouth.

The wise woman builds her house, but with her own hands the foolish one tears hers down. (Proverbs 14:1)

Many years ago I was part of a women's prayer group where we prayed weekly for our unsaved husbands. One of the ground rules set by our leader Cleo was "No husband bashing."

If one of the girls would go off on her husband, Cleo would gently rein her in with something like, "Oh girls, we would never want to say something in this group that would bring dishonor to our husbands." Then she would direct the group's conversation back to prayer.

I so appreciated the example she set. There is definitely a time and a place to have a heart-to-heart with another woman about your marriage troubles, but in a group of twenty-five women, it's not appropriate.

Our mouth can either be a source of blessing and building, or of tearing and ripping. A wise woman will use her mouth to build up her family. Proverbs 10:11 says, "The mouth of the righteous is a fountain of life."

Is your mouth a fountain of life, hope, love, joy, and encouragement? Or are you actually tearing down your own home with the words of your mouth?

Build or tear down? Your choice.

My friend Lori has a great sense of humor and finds something to laugh about in most situations. She's a wonderful storyteller and can entertain and regale a whole dinner party with comical anecdotes all evening.

Lori's husband, John, is often at the center of these funny stories, and is usually content to laugh at his comedic wife along with everyone else. But recently Lori went a little too far. After telling a roomful of people how John accidentally left the phone in the refrigerator, she discovered that sometimes John didn't enjoy being the butt of Lori's jokes. He let her know that divulging his silly blunder to a group of people really embarrassed him.

Now, Lori is a loving and respectful wife. It was never her intention to get laughs at John's expense; it's just that John was always doing funny things!

Women who have a great sense of humor need to be especially careful that they don't tear down their husbands. Lori learned an important lesson from John, and she now tries to be more careful when telling personal stories about him.

Our words are powerful and hold the potential for blessing or cursing. But as in everything, you will have a choice to make. Will you make a determined effort to speak words of life over your husband? Will you build up your home by speaking words of hope and encouragement?

A wise man's heart guides his mouth, and his lips promote instruction. (Proverbs 16:23)

5. Fight for your marriage with change.

The first few years of marriage can be wonderful, difficult, blissful, or challenging. Often it's a combination of all of these things!

My friend ReAnnon is a young woman who is learning to navigate her way through the unique challenges of married life. She is an intelligent and competent woman, and she led an active life as a single girl. She worked full time, traveled the world on mission trips, and held leadership roles wherever she was involved. So, as you can imagine, marriage held a few adjustments for her. One of her biggest adjustments came in the area of money.

She says:

Marriage consists of very little of "mine" and "yours" and a whole lot of "ours." Let me explain.

Before I was married, I had a full-time job and was able to do whatever I wanted with my paycheck. In all honesty, I wasn't very responsible with it. I bought what I wanted when I wanted it. I bought extravagant gifts for those I loved, and I went out to eat A LOT!

But then I got married. And I married a very financially responsible man. A man who valued saving money in a way that was foreign to me. A man who now was completely supporting me because I had enrolled in school full time. I no longer had an income of my own. I no longer had money to do with as I pleased.

After the first several months of marriage I began to resent my husband's frugality. I was torn between wanting to value my husband's wishes and desires regarding finances and my own desires to buy whatever I wanted. I felt like a child. I felt that since I wasn't bringing a paycheck home, that I didn't get a say in what was purchased. I felt like I had to ask permission to buy a soda. However, I was in charge of buying all the groceries, paying all the bills, and keeping track of the checking account. I felt that I lived in a strange monetary paradox: "Be responsible, manage the money, get everything we need, but do it without spending any money." HUH? I grew angry. I wanted freedom to spend money the way I wanted to. I wanted that aspect of my "singleness" back.

It wasn't very long into my marriage that I realized my bitterness was affecting our marriage in a negative way. I had committed to this man for life, and I knew I could not continue in this cycle of bitterness. I sought the Lord and He showed me how I was being very selfish. He showed me how I had overlooked an amazing blessing, and had seen the blessing as a burden. He showed me that He had given me a man who wants to be my provider, a man who doesn't want to live from paycheck to paycheck, and a man who views money differently than I did.

I repented of my selfishness and asked forgiveness for the bitterness I had been carrying. I then decided to change the way I thought about money and how I spent money, with the hope that the way I felt about money would change, too.

As I talked with God daily, He showed me many things. He gave me ideas about how I could serve my husband and his financial vision.

I started buying the Sunday paper and clipping coupons. I turned it into a game—the "How much money did I save today?" game. When I went to the grocery store, I would hold all my coupons until the end. It was a thrill for me to see how much money I saved. Once I saved over $75. It was great!

Another idea God gave me was to meal plan. I started planning a variety of foods and looking forward to what we would be eating for dinner.

The biggest change for me was the way I bought gifts. I began to ask the Lord about what I should purchase for someone. The gifts the Lord suggested were small and sentimental, rather than expensive and impersonal. The recipients of these new kinds of gifts were so much more appreciative than before, and I was spending significantly less money.

Over time the Lord changed me, and my husband noticed the change in my attitude and in the checkbook. He was so appreciative of how I had made the effort to serve him.

Because I changed my actions, the Lord changed my feelings. My view of money and how I spent it was no longer a point of contention in our marriage. The financial vision my husband once held alone, he now shared with me, his wife. I wanted to save money. I wanted to plan for the future. I wanted to live frugally. I wanted to honor the Lord with all that He had given us.

Feelings follow actions, repentance brings change, and communication creates unity.[8]

A Life Well Lived

Like most people, I want to live a meaningful life. It doesn't have to be a great big life involving extreme sports and world travel, but I pray it will be a life that is rich in love and faithfulness. I long to hear the words "Well done, good and faithful servant" when I stand before the Lord at the end of my days.

I think the richness of one's life is found in the small, seemingly insignificant moments of a life well lived. I found this charming article by Katharine Byrne in *Reader's Digest* years ago. It was a great reminder of the absolute grace and simplicity of a good marriage—and of the "richness" that it will add to a woman's life.

You Will Have a Good Life

Alone now much of the time, the widow reads a lot. She used to underline favorite passages to share with her husband. Now, the quotations are stored in a notebook. These lines from Elizabeth Jolley's *Cabin Fever*, for example: "I experience again the deep-felt wish to be part of a married couple, to sit by the fire in winter with the man who is my husband. So intense is this wish that if I write the word *husband* on a piece of paper, my eyes fill with tears."

Why are these lines so painful?

We can start with a worn wedding album. In the first picture, the bride and groom are facing, with uncertain smiles, a church filled with relatives and friends. The bride did not wear glasses that day, so everything was a blur of candlelight, poinsettias, and faces.

They walked to the back of the church and stood at the door as their guests filed past. From colleagues and old schoolmates came cheerful expressions of goodwill clothed in clumsy jokes. Some relatives, however, were not pleased. One sat in a car, sobbing. Another stood surrounded by sympathizers offering condolences. Both of these women—mothers of the bride and groom—would have insisted they wanted only the best for their children. But "the best" they defined as staying home to help support the family.

The last person to approach the couple was a short, sturdy woman who smiled as she congratulated them—not by name, but as "wife" and "husband."

"I'm Aunt Esther Gubbins," she said. "I'm here to tell you that you are going to live a good life and be happy. You will work hard and love each other."

Then quickly, for such a stout and elderly person, she was gone.

Soon they were off, in a borrowed car. With money lent by the groom's brother, they could afford a few days at a state-park lodge. Sitting before a great oak fire, they reviewed the events of the day, remembering the good wishes of their friends, the anguish of their mothers, and the strange message conveyed by Aunt Esther Gubbins.

"Is she your mother's sister or your father's?" asked the wife.

"Isn't she your aunt?" the husband replied. "I never saw her before."

They wondered. Had she come to the wrong church or at the wrong time, mistaking them for another couple? Or was she just an old woman who liked weddings and looked for announcements in the church bulletins?

With the passage of time and the accumulation of grandchildren, their mothers became reconciled to the marriage. One made piles of play clothes for the children; the other crocheted and knitted bonnets, mittens, sweaters, and scarves.

The couple's life together was unremarkable. Oddly, neither ever asked "Whose job is this?" or asserted "That is not my responsibility!" Both acted to fill needs as time and opportunity allowed: groping in the medicine chest for eardrops in the middle of the night to soothe a crying child; tossing in one more load of whites from the perpetual pile at the base of the clothes chute.

Arriving from work, he might stand at the door and announce, "Wife, I am home!" And she, restraining the impulse to let loose a string of well-founded complaints, would call from some corner of the house, "Husband, I am glad!"

Once in a while, usually around their anniversary, they would dredge up the old curiosity regarding Aunt Esther Gubbins. He would insist that the elderly woman had been present at their wedding only accidentally. But she knew that Aunt Esther was on some heavenly mission. At such times, even their children took sides: the earthbound against the fantasists.

Now, alone, the wife asks herself what she would save from the old house if it were to catch fire. Her mother's cameo? Pictures of her husband? The vault key? The $47 hidden in the sugar bowl?

No, it would be the frayed, yellowing envelope she has kept for so long. A woman who spends a lot of time looking for things, she knows exactly where it can be found: under a pile of Madeira napkins used on celebratory occasions.

The husband had fallen asleep in his chair one evening, nodding over a spy novel. She wrote a note on the back of the envelope and left it on his book: "Husband, I have gone next door to help Mrs. Norton figure out her Medicare reimbursements."

The next morning she saw that he had written below her message: "Wife, I missed you. You thought I was asleep, but I was just resting my eyes and thinking about that woman who talked to us in church a long time ago. It has always seemed to me that she was the wrong shape for a heavenly messenger. Anyway, it's time to stop wondering whether she came from heaven or the next parish. What matters is this: Whoever she was, Aunt Esther Gubbins was right."[9]

What Now?

AT THE BEGINNING of this book I invited you on a pilgrimage with me. I warned you that reading it would require a response from you. I challenged you to respond to the "hard stuff" with honesty, transparency, forgiveness, surrender, discovery, and faith.

There were probably a few times during the reading of this book when you leaned toward irritation or frustration, times when you wanted simply to snap the book shut and move on to a nice romance novel (where "real" men quote Wordsworth to their beloved, while picnicking alfresco on verdant fields of green). I'm so glad you didn't! I believe that God is in the business of restoration and regeneration—and that He delights to do this in your marriage.

Hopefully you're finishing your journey with some new insights and tools to facilitate a more joyful, forgiving, and loving marriage. So much of what happens in your future is dependent upon what you do now. The new tools you've received can hang uselessly in the tool shed, or you can begin to pull them out and make progress. Perhaps the most important tool you've received is the spade—used for digging out weeds.

Attack of the Killer Weeds

We recently moved into a smaller home in an effort to downsize and prepare our finances for my husband's impending retirement. Our little house has a planter that skirts the entire length of the home, and it was originally filled with ugly ground cover. This last spring my husband tore out all that ugly ground cover and we replaced it with a vast assortment of flowers. That planter is now a stunning display of color as you drive up to our home. Everyone who visits mentions its beauty. It is thriving, it is flourishing, it is well tended—it is alive!

But that ground cover wants to come back. At first it appears as just a little leafy greenery, but before you know it, it has sent out tentacle-like shoots that begin to insidiously wind their way around and around the stems of the flowers. This stuff is evil! As it winds around each stem, it tightens and slowly chokes the life out of my lovely blossoms.

Every day Jeff or I have to rescue flowers from the "The Attack of the Killer Weeds." If we want our flower garden to continue to thrive and "wow" all the neighbors, then we have to be diligent.

I believe that God has been tending the garden of your marriage while you read this book and examined your marriage by the light of His Word. He has removed some pretty nasty weeds, and has planted some exciting new things in the garden of your marriage. But you'll have to be diligent in your effort not to be overtaken again by the weeds. Remember, the weeds are insidious. At first they appear as benign and non-threatening, but don't be fooled—anything that is *not* a flower does not belong in your garden.

A weed may start off as just a negative memory of something unkind your husband said or did lately. From negative memory to rumination...from rumination to negative emotions...from negative emotions to negative behavior...from negative behavior to resentment. *Bam!* You've got yourself a weed! And it's choking out God's new planting.

Guard against the weeds. Refuse to let them take hold of the good things God has done in your life and marriage. Those negative thought patterns *can* be changed. You don't have to just give up and say, "I can't change; this is just how it is."

With God's help, you can transform long-standing negative patterns in your marriage. He is mighty and will help you keep ugly, joy-stealing weeds out of your garden. Simply do your part, and trust God to do His. Your job is to resist the enemy's plan to steal the good things that God has planted in your marriage; His is to supernaturally strengthen you, giving you His wisdom to overcome each obstacle and keep those weeds out of your garden.

God Will Finish the Good Work He Started

I've been praying for you.

During the writing of this book, I took many long walks and sought God in prayer for the women who would someday read it. I asked Him to do something profound and marvelous in their lives—and in their marriages. And I believe He has.

Many of you started this book in the disconsolate pre-dawn hours of your marriage, but at some point a brilliant sunrise began to unfold. The Lord brought to you a glorious revealing of the man you are married to, and you experienced a true *ta-da!* moment. Don't lose it!

Some of you feel as though you were handed a lifeline by an all-knowing God. He spoke to you in the midst of difficulties and wounds that possibly no other person on earth knows about—reminding you of His promises. He comes to you with whispers of hope—renewing your vision, purpose, and commitment. You now have faith where despair once flourished. Don't lose it!

A few of you have had the hand of God reach down and grasp yours while you were careening toward the precipice of divorce. As you read, you experienced a renewal from the Holy Spirit. And in the middle of what appeared to be complete marital devastation, your hope has been renewed. Your future seems secure (despite your present circumstances) in the hands of the living God. Don't lose it!

Hang on to the lessons you've learned. Hold fast to the things that God has spoken to you. Allow Him to continue the good work He has begun in you. He's not done yet.

Being confident of this, that he who began a good work in you will carry it on to completion until the day of Christ Jesus. (Philippians 1:6)

Some years ago God began a good work in you and your husband. On that day there was shimmering candlelight, romantic music, solemn vows, celebrating, dancing, laughing, and feasting. A bride in white, a groom decked out in a rented tux—you paraded back down the aisle as husband and wife, with smiles as wide as the sea. Everything was right in the world, and the future was brightly anticipated. All was new, all was clean, all was beautiful. The good work had begun.

Let's pray.

❦

Dear Father,

We come to You asking for Your help with our marriages.

We ask You to deepen the love we have for our husbands.

Help us to display Your kindness, faithfulness,

and respect to these men we are married to.

Lord, strengthen us to resist negative thoughts, emotions, and words.

Please help us to forgive our husbands quickly,

and to offer them unconditional love.

We seek You now on behalf of Christian marriages everywhere,

asking that You would stem the tide of divorce.

Forgive us, God, for the ways we have failed.

Rise up on our behalf and purify Your bride, O God.

Wash her with the water of Your Word,

cleanse her from her impurities,

and because of Your mercy, renew her with Your love.

We pray all this in the wonderful and mighty name of Jesus.

Amen.

A Note to the Non-Christian Reader

IF YOU'VE NEVER given your heart and life to Jesus, this is your day! Let's begin by covering a few of the basics.

First, by praying the prayer of salvation you are acknowledging that Jesus Christ is God—that He came to earth as man, lived a sinless life, and died in our place.

Second, you are confessing your sin—living for yourself and not for God.

Third, you are confessing that you are now ready to trust Jesus Christ as Savior and Lord of your life.

If you agree with those three principles, then pray this prayer:

Dear Lord,

I acknowledge that I have broken Your commandments and that my sins have separated me from You.

Please forgive me.

I choose today to turn from my past sinful behavior
and turn toward You. I believe that Your Son, Jesus Christ,
died for my sins, was resurrected from the dead, and is alive!
I invite Jesus to be Lord of my life, and to rule and reign
in my heart from this day forward.
Please, Father, send Your Holy Spirit to help me live for You,
to turn from sin and addiction, and to understand Your Word.
In Jesus' name I pray, amen.

Let's Keep in Touch

Well, ladies…the journey ends here. I have deeply enjoyed the privilege and honor of spending this time with you. I would love to hear from you about how God is working in your life. If you'd like to write me, send an e-mail to:

PFwrites@yahoo.com

Or, you can mail a letter the old-fashioned way to:

Paula Friedrichsen Ministries

P.O. Box 814

Bishop, CA 93514

In addition to being a wife, mom, and writer, I am also a conference speaker. I have developed a seminar based upon the material in this book; it is called "The Man You Always Wanted: A Seminar for Married Women." You can find out more information about this as well as my other seminars by visiting my website:

www.PFMinistries.com

God bless you!

Paula

Notes

1. Geoffrey Cowley, "Halcion—It's the Most Widely Prescribed Sleeping Pill in the World. But is it Safe?" *Newsweek* magazine, August 19, 1991, http://www.injustice.org/nemo/newsfile/nk910819.html (accessed July 11, 2006).
2. Florence Littauer, *Personality Plus* (Grand Rapids, MI: Fleming H. Revell, 1983), 24–27.
3. Shaunti Feldhahn, *For Women Only* (Sisters, OR: Multnomah Publishers, 2003), 99–101.
4. *The NIV Study Bible*, ed., Kenneth Barker (Grand Rapids, MI: Zondervan Bible Publishers), 11.
5. C. S. Lewis, *The Silver Chair* (New York: Collier Books, 1970), 20–21.
6. Jim Killam, "Don't Believe the Divorce Statistics: Why Your Marriage Has Better Than a 50/50 Chance," *Christianity Today International/Marriage Partnership* magazine, Summer 1997, vol. 14, No. 2, 46.
7. Thomas and Nannette Kinkade, *The Many Loves of Marriage* (Sisters, OR: Multnomah Publishers, 2001), 175–77.
8. From personal e-mail correspondence. Used with permission of the author.
9. Katharine Byrne, "You Will Have a Good Life," *Reader's Digest* magazine, condensed from "America" by Katharine Byrne. This article first appeared in *Reader's Digest* on November 14, 1992. Used with permission of the author.